BLESSED SURVIVOR

My Journey From Survival Of Attempted Murder And Rape To A Purpose Filled Life

By Rhonda Knight

PURPOSE FILLED LIFE

BLESSED SURVIVOR

BLESSED SURVIVOR

My Journey from survival of attempted murder and rape to a purpose filled life

ISBN-10: 0615449859
ISBN-13: 978-0615449852 (Lady Knight Enterprises Publishing)

Cover Design inspired by God and Art Work created by Rhonda Knight

All quoted biblical scriptures are from the King James Version.

PURPOSE FILLED LIFE

DEDICATION

This book is dedicated with love

to the children of God

and to

My lovely daughters-Mignon, Amber, Alicia, Jasmyn and Kayla

and to

My awesome parents, George and Connie

I LOVE YOU!

INTRODUCTION

Because of what I've experienced and the battles, struggles and challenges to overcome this tragedy, is one of the reasons why I feel lead to help other women who are also blessed survivors like me. I want to be instrumental in helping them to be overcomers, to have uplifted hearts, minds and souls. I know this is what I needed in this healing journey and I know that doing this by the grace of God, is the driving force and fuel that gives me strength to go on………

As I write I hear a word from God…

This book is also written for anyone who needs healing, deliverance, guidance, peace and renewing of their spirit. I also hear this book is for those in ministry, whether for their own personal struggles, needs or healing; or for those chosen to use this knowledge and Godly inspired wisdom to help in their ministry in leading those who are hurt to walk in God's love, grace and peace.

Blessed Survivor

To Greg & Regina

May you continue to prosper & bless you two and may you be a blessing to others in your work!

Rhonda Knight

Blessed Survivor

CONTENTS

BLESSED SURVIVOR

FOREWORD

This book is a must read because it ministers to those who are bound, stuck at a place of fear, guilt and shame. From pain to a purpose filled life is a powerful testimony to how God can turn what the devil meant for evil around for your good. This book may cause you to weep as you read page after page while thinking about all this woman of God had been through and was going through as she transcends from pain to a purpose filled life. This story and testimony shows you that if you hold on to your belief in God as Rhonda did from the beginning of her ordeal, how God is so faithful and loving that He will provide a way of escape and also to know that what can be too hard for us is not too hard for God.

Minister Larry Jones-Love and Faith, Chaplain of Minister Alliance at Changing A Generation Full Gospel Baptist Church where the Pastors are Bishop Paul S. Morton and Co-Pastor Debra B. Morton

BLESSED SURVIVOR

CHAPTER 1

THE "FRIENDSHIP"

How it all started…

I had befriended a man around the end of November in 2005. He was a man who had a much different background and lifestyle than I. I am foremost a woman who loves God! I am one who is very enthusiastic, optimistic, caring, nice and a happy-go-lucky person who has a very big heart.

I love people and have always wanted to reach out and help anyone who needed help. I have been blessed to have five beautiful Daughters, two of which I adopted and four wonderful handsome Grandsons along with my first gorgeous Granddaughter and now a second lovely Granddaughter on the way!.

I am a business minded person that has also been blessed with a creative side in the Arts as well. My family background is one that operates in love.

I don't smoke nor do I do drugs and only once in a while will I have a mixed drink or glass of wine, I don't care for the taste of alcohol. My immediate family is the same way. In addition strive to live a Christian lifestyle. He on the other then and also used drugs. He would say and he sold drugs was on drugs or alcoholics. also told me most of his grew up in the "hood" as he

We met in a rather way; it was at the drive-thru of a White Castle resta cut and muscular guy. My second oldest Daughter worked there; he appeared to be a polite, handsor decided to play matchmaker against my protests. When he returned to the window, she asked him if he was single. He said yes, my Daughter said so is my Mom! I was soooo embarrassed! He handed out his phone number and asked me to call him. I didn't call at first, because for one thing I was still quite embarrassed and secondly I'm not accustomed to meeting people that way. Then one day I did call, we talked. He invited me out to a movie; I went even though I was experiencing severe back pain at the time.

Have you ever been on a date trying to look cute but you are having so much pain that you really want to hold on to anything and everything or grab a cane, walker or something! But instead you just smile and pretend that everything is ok. Well that was the case for me, so I set through the movie and of all times it happened to be a three hour movie! Well thus was the beginning of the so called friendship.

After the movie we went to dinner and we talked. He told me about his past and that he was a recovering crack addict and that's why at his age he had taken a job at White Castle. He also told me that he was involved in a horrible accident in Chicago, (which is his hometown) he said during that time, he had just left their family reunion and that he and his girlfriend were arguing over money pertaining to wanting to get more drugs. He said he was driving very fast on the expressway and lost control of the car. The car flipped over about eighteen times, he was told, before hitting a car on the opposite side of the expressway. The driver of that car was killed, and others injured. He and his girlfriend lived, obtaining only minor injuries. He said in regards to his arrest, he first decided to flee. While hiding out, he spoke his Mother who talked him into turning himself in. He ended up doing three years in prison. He said that it really bothered him that he killed someone... How ironic.

Because he had been somewhat honest with me from the start and the fact that I was not a judgmental person, our different background and lifestyles, I'd decided regardless of which lead to us eventually dating. After talking know him better know him through our dating, I realized this man had getting to issues!

PURPOSE FILLED LIFE

Before I realized those issues we seemed to be developing a good friendship. We started going to church together, which mostly was my church. He had his own church home, but liked the ministry and teaching God brings through my Pastor. He'd emphasize to us that it is neither about him as Pastor nor about you as an individual. The picture is much bigger than that, it is really all about Jesus Christ, Yahshua and what he did on the cross, and that the answers to life all lay within the cross. When you come to an understanding about that, you will then be able to live a full blessed life where you don't have to seek miracles because your life needs are met. Your faith, trust and understanding of who He is and what it is you are here to do is clear. You then walk in that place of total kingdom living of a blessed life!

You see we have to learn how to walk in that grace and seek the Lord in regards to our purpose and His will for our lives. This is where my heart is, it is what I'm back to doing now, this is where I am heading in my journey to complete healing and a purpose filled life. It is the path I was on prior to meeting.......his real last name is a color, however for this book, I'm going to change it to another color; BLACK, because of the darkness he caused in my life. Black was a distraction to me. During the time we met, I was looking forward to going into ministry training at my church. I was already a licensed Evangelist when I started attending this church. However I didn't walk in this calling in the tradition sense there at my new church home. I humbly and gladly worshipped and served as an usher. Of course I still continued to allow God to use me in ministry which included the women's ministry I oversaw that was formed before my divorce from my ex Husband with whom I shared ҅ԁ a small church. I willingly allowed God to use me in ҅aw fit. A title is not what is important in life; it's ҅alling.

҅ church to grow in my
҅ike everything
҅ain or
҅at

particular endeavor, so of course I wanted to be the very best that I could be for God.

I admired my Pastors' approach to God's word because he would study a subject for years sometimes before presenting it to the congregation. He'd often write college style paper reports on it as well. Then he'd stay on that subject Sunday after Sunday until he thought we really understood it or until God lead him to the next subject. I felt privileged to have a chance to train under such a humble deeply committed Pastor like Pastor Lane.

I had went up that June of 2005 to accept the calling to train, but had not attended at our church long enough at that time, based on our church's guidelines. So I had to wait until January 2006 at which point I was accepted, however our training classes would not begin until September 2007. I trained there up until June of 2008 then we had a summer break with classes scheduled to resume in September. But before I continue here, I want to go back to my story that leads to this journey in this season of my life.

I ended up at the hospital on Christmas day 2005 because my back went all the way out; I couldn't move and was in excruciating pain. I don't remember what the Doctor said it was but they gave me some pain medication that knocked me out and the next day I was good as new! 2006 came in and I continued to date Black. I had just started working for a mortgage company when we met and was trying to build up clientele. In that process I got behind on my rent and had to move. Black was staying in a ¾ house and had a disagreement with another man there and was being put out.

I want to tell you about what I saw in Black at that time. I saw a young man who really wanted to know God and who had a gift of talking to people and in his own way, encouraging them. I believe that Black had a calling on his life to reach those who had been where he had been. But I also believe that we as individuals have to accept that calling and walk in it. Black made a decision to turn the other way as you'll read later. I also saw a perso saddened by his family's extensive

CHAPTER 1

THE "FRIENDSHIP"

How it all started...

I had befriended a man around the end of November in 2005. He was a man who had a much different background and lifestyle than I. I am foremost a woman who loves God! I am one who is very enthusiastic, optimistic, caring, nice and a happy-go-lucky person who has a very big heart.

I love people and have always wanted to reach out and help anyone who needed help. I have been blessed to have five beautiful Daughters, two of which I adopted and four wonderful handsome Grandsons along with my first gorgeous Granddaughter and now a second lovely Granddaughter on the way!.

I am a business minded person that has also been blessed with a creative side in the Arts as well. My family background is one that operates in love.

I don't smoke nor do I do drugs and only once in awhile will I have a mixed drink or glass of wine, I don't care for the taste of alcohol. My immediate family is the same way. I, in addition strive to live a Christian lifestyle. He on the other hand, grew up in the "hood" as he would say and he sold drugs back then and also used drugs. He also told me most of his family was on drugs or alcoholics.

We met in a rather strange way; it was at the drive-thru of a White Castle restaurant. He worked there; he appeared to be a polite, handsome, clean cut and muscular guy. My second oldest Daughter decided to play matchmaker against my protests. When he returned to the window, she asked him if he was single. He said yes, my Daughter said so is my Mom! I was soooo embarrassed! He handed out his phone number and asked me to call him. I didn't call at first, because for one thing I was still quite embarrassed and secondly I'm not accustomed to meeting people that way. Then one day I did call, we talked. He invited me out to a movie; I went even though I was experiencing severe back pain at the time.

Have you ever been on a date trying to look cute but you are having so much pain that you really want to hold on to anything and everything or grab a cane, walker or something! But instead you just smile and pretend that everything is ok. Well that was the case for me, so I set through the movie and of all times it happened to be a three hour movie! Well thus was the beginning of the so called friendship.

After the movie we went to dinner and we talked. He told me about his past and that he was a recovering crack addict and that's why at his age he had taken a job at White Castle. He also told me that he was involved in a horrible accident in Chicago, (which is his hometown) he said during that time, he had just left their family reunion and that he and his girlfriend were arguing over money pertaining to wanting to get more drugs. He said he was driving very fast on the expressway and lost control of the car. The car flipped over about eighteen times, he was told, before hitting a car on the opposite side of the expressway. The driver of that car was killed, and others injured. He and his girlfriend lived, obtaining only minor injuries. He said in regards to his arrest, he first decided to flee. While hiding out, he spoke to his Mother who talked him into turning himself in. He ended up doing three years in prison. He said that it really bothered him that he killed someone…How ironic.

Because he had been somewhat honest with me from the start and the fact that I was not a judgmental person, I decided regardless of our different background and lifestyles, I'd get to know him better which lead to us eventually dating. After talking to him and getting to know him through our dating, I realized this man had a lot of issues!

Before I realized those issues we seemed to be developing a good friendship. We started going to church together, which mostly was my church. He had his own church home, but liked the ministry and teaching God brings through my Pastor. He'd emphasize to us that it is neither about him as Pastor nor about you as an individual. The picture is much bigger than that, it is really all about Jesus Christ, Yahshua and what he did on the cross, and that the answers to life all lay within the cross. When you come to an understanding about that, you will then be able to live a full blessed life where you don't have to seek miracles because your life needs are met. Your faith, trust and understanding of who He is and what it is you are here to do is clear. You then walk in that place of total kingdom living of a blessed life!

You see we have to learn how to walk in that grace and seek the Lord in regards to our purpose and His will for our lives. This is where my heart is, it is what I'm back to doing now, this is where I am heading in my journey to complete healing and a purpose filled life. It is the path I was on prior to meeting.......his real last name is a color, however for this book, I'm going to change it to another color; BLACK, because of the darkness he caused in my life. Black was a distraction to me. During the time we met, I was looking forward to going into ministry training at my church. I was already a licensed Evangelist when I started attending this church. However I didn't walk in this calling in the tradition sense there at my new church home. I humbly and gladly worshipped and served as an usher. Of course I still continued to allow God to use me in ministry which included the women's ministry I oversaw that was formed before my divorce from my ex Husband with whom I shared overseeing a small church. I willingly allowed God to use me in whatever way He saw fit. A title is not what is important in life; it's what you do with that gift or calling.

There was an opportunity presented at my church to grow in my calling through a four year period of training. Just like everything else I'd set my mind to do in life, I'd always read books, train or obtain other knowledge on the subject so that I would excel at that particular endeavor, so of course I wanted to be the very best that I could be for God.

I admired my Pastors' approach to God's word because he would study a subject for years sometimes before presenting it to the congregation. He'd often write college style paper reports on it as well. Then he'd stay on that subject Sunday after Sunday until he thought we really understood it or until God lead him to the next subject. I felt privileged to have a chance to train under such a humble deeply committed Pastor like Pastor Lane.

I had went up that June of 2005 to accept the calling to train, but had not attended at our church long enough at that time, based on our church's guidelines. So I had to wait until January 2006 at which point I was accepted, however our training classes would not begin until September 2007. I trained there up until June of 2008 then we had a summer break with classes scheduled to resume in September. But before I continue here, I want to go back to my story that leads to this journey in this season of my life.

I ended up at the hospital on Christmas day 2005 because my back went all the way out; I couldn't move and was in excruciating pain. I don't remember what the Doctor said it was but they gave me some pain medication that knocked me out and the next day I was good as new! 2006 came in and I continued to date Black. I had just started working for a mortgage company when we met and was trying to build up clientele. In that process I got behind on my rent and had to move. Black was staying in a ¾ house and had a disagreement with another man there and was being put out.

I want to tell you about what I saw in Black at that time. I saw a young man who really wanted to know God and who had a gift of talking to people and in his own way, encouraging them. I believe that Black had a calling on his life to reach those who had been where he had been. But I also believe that we as individuals have to accept that calling and walk in it. Black made a decision to turn the other way as you'll read later. I also saw a person who was saddened by his family's extensive use of drugs mostly but alcohol too. Especially his oldest Sister who he'd say used to be so pretty to him but now she looked deathly skinny with sunken in eyes as if she were the walking dead. A result of being strung out on crack.

I had the opportunity to visit with his family at their holiday gatherings and was saddened at how many of them would show up at his Grandparent's house for dinner extremely high off crack or very drunk and everybody would ignore it. The part that really saddened me was watching the children who saw this lifestyle as the norm. And I prayed that they would not grow up thinking this was their destiny too. Unfortunately, this is what happened with Black. He told me how he saw his Aunts and Uncles messed up from using and said he wasn't going to be like them but ended up using and abusing drugs anyway. He talked about not wanting to go back to that lifestyle and that he remembered how his Nieces and Nephews looked at him then. He hated those times in his life, times where he too looked like death walking and was so skinny himself from being strung out.

His Mother was the exception; she did not use drugs nor was she an alcoholic. She was a retired nurse who also did foster care. Her second or third Husband (not Black's Father) also at a point used crack but Black said he thought he was clean in these days. She was always kind to me and seemed to really love her children even though it broke her heart that out of the four biological children she had, three had been crack addicts and one was a weed head who drank and partied with a lot of men.

His Grandparents were nice to me as well. I only met his Brother who still lived in Chicago, on one occasion at his Grandparents and of course he was high and probably doesn't even remember meeting me. His other Sister who was the weed smoker was raising her Granddaughter who is a cute and smart little petite girl. Her Daughter who was the Mother of this little girl died after falling down the stairs while very pregnant, she had pneumonia and had blacked out and fell. She and the baby she carried died. She laid there on the floor until found while her very young Daughter went unattended, too young to understand what had happened to her

Mommy. That death really affected his Sister and himself, I know because one night he cried so hard as he recalled the story and relayed it to me. This Sister was nice towards me as well and I enjoyed talking to her on the few times we spoke. She didn't see herself as having a problem like her siblings.

I also had met his oldest Sister who despite her addiction, seemed to love children and was raising a family member's child and would often babysit other children in the family, high or not. She never had any children of her own. She would tell me funny stories of them growing up and how Black was a Momma's boy, spoiled by his Mom and by her. I could tell she really loved her siblings. I thought to myself that if she hadn't gotten strung out she'd be a good Mother as I watched her cook and later do her given Daughter's hair. I also witnessed how she kept a clean neat house and ironed and folded her Niece's clothes that she babysat for. That same older Sister had been hospitalized from over dosing and had died for a few minutes until the Doctors revived her. He was so furious with her because as soon as she got back home she was out their again buying alcohol and crack.

I want to continue on in regards to my having to move and Black having too also. We decided to share a two bed motel room. Now before you become judgmental, one thing I did appreciate about Black at the time was he for the most part respected my not wanting to be intimate with him.

I will say that prior to our staying at the motel and during our brief dating period, I did have a weak moment and we did get intimate. Afterward I cried and cried because I hated that I even got weak at all and I really hated letting God down which is what I felt I did. Here I was trying to focus on my ministry and then I went there. I am so critical of myself when I feel I failed. I don't convict myself, I condemn myself. This is not what our heavenly Father wants from us. It is a trick of the enemy. God knows that we will fall short, but when we do, we should feel convicted, not condemned. This is what humbles us and gives us the desire to want to repent and ask for forgiveness, knowing that our gracious and merciful Father will forgive us.

Another trick is that we have to believe God really did forgive us and not keep beating ourselves up about it which is what the enemy wants us to do. I say this here because I have to try very hard to forgive myself. I want to be the best for God and give Him my best. Every gift or talent or project I have learned or set my mind to do, I learn all I can and read, study, practice or follow the instructor or instructions etc. I like to be the best and I like perfection in my work, so as I mentioned earlier, if I am this way with everything else then I definitely want to be this way for God.

I once talked to a very spiritually wise Brother and friend of mine in regards of feeling like a hypocrite if I went to church and worshipped and praised God when I may have had some wrong thoughts or if I had sinned. I felt it would be being a fake. He said are you faking it when you are praising and worshipping or really doing it? I said I am really worshipping and praising Him. He said then you are not faking it. I said but I'd rather not even go to church if my thoughts aren't right, like I said I feel like a hypocrite sitting there. He went on to say how that is the very time you need to be there, where God can lead and guide you through His word, where He can remind you that He loves you in spite of yourself.

You see the enemy uses our condemnation to get us to turn away from God because of our guilt. But you defeat the enemy when you press forward and still give God the glory by going to church and by privately and publicly loving on God in your own time of communion with Him. I'm not about to give the enemy any chances to trick me if I can help it so I learned to stay in God's presence when I'm not feeling so good about myself and He surely gets me back to where I need to be!

As I am writing this book, please keep in mind that I write then stop and days, months or even years may pass. So there may be times that I share my thoughts and feelings at that present time that may make it seem like I'm contradicting my earlier faith statements.

Remember this is a healing journey so you will be on this roller coaster of my emotions, struggles, extreme sadness, brief happy moments, the "I can't go on, I'm a failure moments" and most importantly the "I'M HEALED" moment. But please know that through it all, the good and the bad times, deep in my heart, even deep down in my spirit, I know I will survive and be victorious!

There is also a reason God had you read this book. Therefore, as you read search your heart and ask God to reveal to you what he wants you to receive from the message in this book.

Now back to where I left off, Black seemed to be doing well that is until he had received his income tax return. This was right after his oldest Sister had got out of the hospital. We went by her house to visit her and she was high already. Black was so upset and mad after we left. He said he can't understand how she could go back to using when she just died in the hospital and had to be resuscitated. Within that same week he too went back to smoking crack. He came in one day looking so crazy and out of it. His eyes were glazed over, he couldn't keep still, his face was twitching, he appear very robotic like to me. He also was very slow in his responses; he had a difficult time trying to speak. Even though I had never seen anyone high off crack that up close and personal, I knew that was what was going on. I immediately was upset with him. I told him he needed to call and get back into a program right away. At that point he was in no condition to follow those instructions. When he finally came down, he enrolled back in a program. His using again was not acceptable to me, so I ended our short dating relationship. I had been working hard at trying to build my career so that my family and I could live a better and more comfortable life. I also was not going to allow anyone to hinder my goal to live a righteous lifestyle which I was trying to do as well.

I kept the friendship however, because he would sometimes talk about suicide. Being a Christian I felt it would be wrong to turn my back on someone who has been contemplating suicide. I had also taken a class on suicide when I trained in drama therapy. The instructor told us that when a person tells you they contemplated suicide believe them and reach out and help them if you can; she went on to say that it is a myth that if someone tells you then they are not really serious and won't commit suicide.

So as I mentioned I kept the friendship especially since I saw him go back into rehab and that he was trying to conquer this demon. He was fine with us just being friends. Over the next year and a half of our friendship, we would go through ups and downs as friends sometimes do. We'd also share some fun times and some very intense times as I tried to help him in his battle with crack.

I remember one time in particular when we were at a mutual friends' house where Black had been staying. Well I noticed he was getting antsy and I knew something was up. He had called the dope dealer and asked him to bring him some crack to the house; of course he didn't tell me that. He went outside and I followed him, which he protested against but his hunger to get that rock made him stop trying to argue with me and get to that car with the drugs. I'm following him trying to talk some sense into his head but he is ignoring me. As he approaches the car I start threatening the people in the car. "I'm gonna call the Police! I got your license plate number; you better not give that to him!" Etc. they get hesitant, he's telling them to ignore me, they're not sure what to do, then finally they give him the drugs! I'm so mad that I take the beer can out of his hand and throw it at their car while they're pulling off.

Now I know this was really, really dumb behavior, I could have gotten beaten up, shot or killed. Here's where I want you to understand what I seen with my own eyes and also learned about crack addiction from Black. This man when sober would absolutely with his whole heart desire to stay clean. Remember when I told you about him being very mad at his Sister but yet that same week he went and used, well he told me that when he saw his Sister he could smell the crack on her and that trigger is what sent him off on a crack binge. As much as he hated seeing her like that and knowing she died and the fact it could kill him too was not enough to stop the stronghold crack had on him. I seen this grown man cry and pour out his heart about wanting to stay clean. He told me when you're a fiend for crack you don't care about anything or anybody. Your mind is totally obsessed with getting that drug. He shared how bad he felt especially for hurting his Mom by using crack. I happened to know this man totally loved and adored his Mom. But even that love alone was not enough to make him get total control over this addiction. He'd have periods of doing well then he'd slip back out there. I saw him at least trying where from what he told me, his older Sister and his Brother refused to get help from any program or anybody.

Moving on, I had worked my way up in business. I went to a different mortgage company who offered me my own branch to solely operate and run and in a short period my branch became the number two most producing branch out of eleven and I was the number one in personal loans produced throughout the company. I also had started my own property management company. I was doing well in business and was able to move to West Bloomfield, Michigan a very well to do community where the majority of the people who lived here were from old money. As a single Mom and business woman, all my years of hard work was finally paying off…

Yes, things were looking up! I had a great group of people who worked for me and had developed new friendships, some of which I still have. I had money in the bank, the kind of car I wanted, a 2800 square foot, two story condo style apartment and a healthy happy family! It's not about the material things but we all want to live comfortably and most parents want to build a financially successful business or build up their finances so that their children and their children's children can have a prosperous life. Prosperous from a physical standpoint and also from a spiritual standpoint from the seeds we as parents have successfully sown in our children by the grace of God.

I had once taken Black with me to a business associate and dear friend's house for a meeting and to loan another friend who was there, my projector. He had a lovely three story condo and welcomed us into his home. They were very nice to Black and treated him as if they had known him all along. On the drive back Black was very irate. As he was driving my car he started raving on about my friends. He said they think they're something because they have a baby grand piano in their living room and because they got money and he went on and on in a jealous fit. I told him these guys were not those kind of people, they are humble down to earth guys and that they were genuinely nice to him and really liked him. He then told me that he'd crash my car into a wall on the expressway. We argued all the way to his house that day. Black normally would always ask me could he go with me to this meeting or that meeting and loved getting involved in the things I was doing. He'd also like to brag to his family and friends about what we did or where we went. So his behavior that day caught me off guard, I think it was more of a male ego type thing.

One of the other things Black would like to do is accompany me when I went to show my clients' property in the Detroit or Ecorse area so that I would not be a woman showing property alone with strangers and sometimes in a questionable neighborhood.

I would periodically do gospel play productions and was working on one we'd run several times. It is an awesome play written by one of my best friends, William E. Smith who's also a very wise, "Solomon in the bible" wise type of guy. I performed one of the lead roles and also Co-Directed this production. I was also the Technical Director of the show. One Saturday morning in the dead of winter I was preparing to gather all the props for the show and pack them in my car. Black was over and was assisting me.

I have an American Eskimo dog that I absolutely love and adore. His name is Snow; he is a medium small size dog, white in color with a light biscuit coloring along his back. I'm crazy about this dog because I prayed one day and asked God to please give me a dog, I need a puppy to love I prayed. And through a stranger that I met in a Red Lobster restaurant I ended up getting him. This lady had saw me at a dog adoption fair earlier that day and happened to run into me again at Red Lobster. I didn't remember seeing her but she asked me if I had gotten a dog. I told her that I saw an American Eskimo that I wanted but the people said I couldn't have him. Months passed and this woman called Red Lobster and talked to my friend who was a Manager there and told her she had a dog for me.

When I got Snow I thanked God, Snow was like a Guardian Angel to me and a beautiful gift from God! He is the kind of dog whose whole life is set on pleasing me, if he gets in trouble he will try to never make me upset again. He follows me to whatever room I go to then he will sit there and guard the door to protect me. He is also my "non violence" dog as I call him, he will not let you argue or fuss in front of him. If the kids are arguing or if I fuss too loud at them, he will bark and jump up on you to say stop. He is a very smart, loyal and loving dog.

Well this day as we were preparing to leave, Black went to let Snow outside. He went downstairs to my lower level that had a patio door that lead out to my backyard with the frozen lake in the distant feet away. He proceeded to tie the expandable leash to the door of the patio and allow Snow to go do his business. That was fine with me because it was way too cold out for anyone to be standing out there waiting for him to finish. Black came back up to finish helping me, the problem was that Black didn't secure the door properly so when we came back down to get Snow he was gone... I'm yelling outside on the patio, Snooooow, snooooow and so is he.

Where my place was situated was very close to the road in front of my unit and then surrounded by trees on the side. There were woods everywhere to the side of the home and in back. Beyond the lake were 100's of other condo style apartments and more woods throughout that whole community, with frozen over lakes, creeks and hills too.

I'm panicky now because my baby is lost and I have a show opening very soon that I have to get to. I've got all the props and I also need to make sure the Lighting and Sound Techs have everything correct and that my Stage Crew is properly prepared and that everything is set up and in place. All the things I have to do prior to the production and then have enough time to get ready myself to perform. But I can't leave my dog lost out there freezing and in danger of getting hit by a car. Black goes searching for Snow, but he can't find him. I'm getting more and more upset to the point of crying. Neighbors hear us and ask if we have a child missing, I say no it's my dog.

We search the lake to make sure he didn't some how fall in through a crack or something. I'm still calling Snow...then I hear something in the far distance, it sounds like a dog barking, could it be Snow, I pray it is. We can't tell were the sound is coming from, it echoes off the solid hard snow. Black takes off in the cold to follow the barks of distress. He feels guilty for not securing the door properly and says he's sorry. I keep yelling Snow's name so he will keep barking. I'm hoping that it's him and not some other dog probably barking trying to tell us "SHUT UP HUMANS".

He finally finds him way down an embankment near the creek, his leash tangled in the trees. I see him and Snow coming in the distance, I'm so happy and relieved, my baby and gift from God is alive and ok! Thank God he found him or he surely would have frozen to death out there tangled up. Everybody who knows me knows I'm crazy about that dog and Black told me he knew he had to find him for me. That was the kindest thing Black had done for me, he was my hero that day and I appreciated it; that's why I had to add this story in my book. By the way I arrived a little late to the theatre but the show started on time without any issues.

In May of 2007 I drove Black to Chicago to see his Mother on Mother's day and to spend a couple of days there. I visited my Mom the day before we left and gave her the gifts I had gotten her. I then kissed her all up like I always do. I explained to her that I was going to drive Black there because I know how he had been missing his Mom and that he was concerned even more now about her health. Because the last time she came to Michigan to visited her Mother and family, she ended up being rushed to the hospital with an entirely different medical concern. She was ecstatic to see her Son. I met some more of his family members and we visited downtown Chi town while we were there. Less than a month later he would try to kill me.

13

I have shared these things with you in this chapter to paint a picture for you of what I thought was a genuine friendship. I was not only like this with Black; I showed all my friends this kind of love, support and kindness. Hopefully you will now understand why my guards were down with Black. Even though he had done some kind acts too, this man would later turn into a hideous demonized monster…

CHAPTER 2

JUNE 2007 THE BEGINNING OF THE END OF A "FRIENDSHIP" AND ALMOST THE END OF A LIFE

On Sunday, June 3rd, 2007 I told Black that I keep hearing this voice, which I believe is the Holy Spirit saying, God wants me to stay focused and wants me to get negativity out of my life. I thought about that and I came to the conclusion that everyone around me was positive, optimistic people and the only negativity in any form in my life was Black and he was also a distraction at times. He was a person who had many, many issues in life and he had allowed those things to make him into a very negative and bitter person, never really towards me but about life in general. He complained about hating his job and the Indian people who worked there. He often would go on about this person or that person at work and that he felt the Indians who worked there just looked out for each other. He expressed his dislike of so many things which included his Mother being in Chicago, not having the things he wanted in life and the list goes on.

In my breaking this news to him, I was very kind and compassionate toward him. I also tried to encourage him to stay faithful and keep trusting God in everything. I firmly expressed to him that this was something that I have to do and no offense to him but I have to be obedient.

I would also share with Black and others that I felt that I was going to be instrumental in bringing a lot of people together but not for the reason they thought, it was going to be because God desires to show His people how much He loves them. I had the opportunity to bring people in business at the time and still do in this present time with another company, but if that was it, it was not going to be about the business I'd say then and still continue to say now.

I would also say that it was going to be something very big, like if you were looking at the ocean then this was going to be like the size of a tsunami not just an ordinary wave. I kept hearing this…

In the week to follow, Black called my house, cell phone and office over and over even though I asked him not too, so I had to resort to not answering or accepting his calls. I was staying true to what I'd said to him. He also had his Mother call me. She and I talked and I told her the same thing I had told Black.

The following Sunday, June 10th, I got up and attended church. We had a visiting Pastor from Chicago who was bringing the message. The Pastor says to the congregation "God wants you to get negativity out of your life" wow confirmation to what I was hearing. He said those murderers or victims. Strangely, I would have been murdered and a victim. His meaning was about those people who "murder" your visions, dreams or faith etc. or those who are always the "victim" where everyone and everything is against them in their eyesight.

The Pastor went on to say be careful of what you say, as he referenced it to a scripture that tells how powerful our words are. An example he gave is like if I sneeze then say "oh I'm catching a cold" well then my body would say, Rhonda says she's catching a cold so stand down and let her catch it. Be careful what you say he said… service ended and I decided to head over to my new office.

At this time I had selected to become partners in business with two associates of mine. We decided to combine our offices. So I was moving some of my things from my other office to the new location throughout that week. I had to let my personal assistant go temporarily until we could finish getting situated in the new place. Needless to say I had to do all the things she usually did to get me in preparation for the week ahead.

As I was working Black phoned me again so this time I took the call. He starts to talk about our situation, when I speak I remind him that in the year and a half I've known him, he had not changed and I know that God wants me to stay focused and get rid of all negativity. "Can we still go to dinner sometimes or to a movie" he asked. No Black that would be the same things we'd already sometimes do, I replied. I also told Him that I was not trying to be mean, but I know what I have to do. I expressed to him that he was acting too dependent on me and that he needed to trust God more. I always try to redirect people back to God when I'm helping or encouraging an individual because I never want anyone to look at Rhonda and give me the credit for anything. I know how easy it is for some people to see a human as the answer, so I constantly try to remind whoever it is to look to the true source of their help which is God, not me, I'm just an instrument. I went on to tell him that I know that God will take care of him just like He takes care of me.

I also said to him, I hope you didn't go back to using drugs because you've been upset. He said no he didn't and that would I please let him prove it to me. He said he wants to show me he has changed and would I please come and "drop" him (take a urine sample and test it for drugs). You see, in my Property Management company I spoke with some of my property Owners and shared with them the benefit of having their rental property utilized to help recovering women transitioning back into society. I explained that these women needed a temporary place to stay in their last step before returning to their own residence. Black knew I managed these types of homes which are called ¾ homes; remember he too had also stayed in these types of homes for men on occasion and he is the reason I had knowledge about them. An important part of managing these homes is to assure everyone staying there stays clean (drug free) which means you have to conduct periodic drops. So of course he knew that I knew how to do this and thus asked me to test him. He kept insisting until I finally said ok, but I told him if he was clean then that's great! It means you are finally trusting God completely and seeing that you can stay strong. However, I made it clear to him that this was not going to change my decision about us.

I ended up staying way later then I had planned. When I left I headed towards home it was around midnight. I phoned my mom and spoke with her as I drove towards my place. I got about a mile from home before I remembered that I'd promised him I'd come by, take him to CVS to get the kit and then drop him. Even though I was tired, I wanted to keep my promise. I ended the call with my mom, telling her I forgot I was supposed to do something first before I went home. I then headed back on the freeway to his apartment.

When I arrived, I called his cell to tell him I was in the parking lot. He came out, got in the car and stared out of the window. He seemed preoccupied and distant. When we got to the store, he was out of the car and in the store at the register before I could even get out of the car and into the store. I had just barely made it in there as he was paying for the kit. He was very quiet and unusually calm. I thought, well maybe he thinks if he's silent and if he has a different demeanor, I'll change my mind…maybe that's what he's thinking…I don't know. What I did not know was that he was luring me over to his house under false pretenses.

Once we got back to his place, he said he needed to drink some water because he didn't feel like he could use the bathroom. I told him I was tired and needed to get home and would he please try to go. He went into the bathroom, came out and said I told you I couldn't go yet.

He headed toward his bedroom. You see he didn't make much money and had only recently got a place of his own. However he couldn't furnish it yet so the majority of furniture he had was a bed, a chair and a small TV that sat on a stand, which were all in his bedroom. He sat on the end of the bed and cut on his television. I sat in the chair near the end of the bed. As I sat down there, I started to talk to him, when all of a sudden he turned toward me and started nonstop punching me in my face, in shock, pain, fear and disbelief I asked him what he was doing, he says he did not bring me here for the reason I thought, he says he brought me there to kill me then himself and that the only way we were going to leave there was in body bags. He says he was going to slit my throat then his.

As he is beating my face, he knocks me out of the chair and onto the floor. I don't know where he had his knife, all I know is he did and he was punching me in the face with all this rage and anger and trying to kill me by cutting my throat. He was yelling things like "he couldn't eat or sleep" and that "he'd been crying every night and that I was going on with my life" he even took all the things I said about God and threw them back in my face verbally.

At some point as I lay on the floor with him over me, he slices my left arm open just over my elbow, it's a deep gaping wound... and he also cuts me all the way across my right hand and there is a stab wound in my upper inner right arm area.

He stabs me in my left eye, I feel the blade go directly into my eyeball and out I say oh my God, you stabbed me in my eye! He says I don't care I'm going to kill you! I thought that any minute my eye was going to gush out fluids and or deflate or something.

Every movie or story I had heard about people getting stabbed in the eye with any object, especially with something as sharp as a knife, they would die or definitely lose the eye... I'm going to be blind, fluids are going to start gushing out...I'm going to lose my eye...or worse, I whisper, I'm going to die...

He did a fast cut across my throat but miraculously my throat did not slice open like my arm and hand did. I knew he owned this knife (which has about a 3 inch blade) and I knew he kept it very sharp because he would sometimes use it at his job. I never knew he'd use it as a weapon against me...

I keep thinking that God warned me and here I am about to die in this room tonight. I thought I was being obedient, I was just going to do this last favor...I'm going to die, I don't want to die, help me God...I don't want to die...

I could feel my face swelling from the blows that kept coming and coming... My hands and arms looked deformed just like my face was now looking. The deformities are from all the blows that missed my face but struck my arms as I held them up in protection of my face and throat.

I tried begging and pleading with him to no avail. SHUT UP, SHUT UP! He'd yell...it's to late for all that!

I'm so terrified, I'm looking into the eyes of this man who doesn't look anything like the man I knew...he looks possessed...his eyes, his eyes are so dark, demonic, so terrifying...

Oh my God! I'm going to die ...I'm going to die!

He is steadily trying to cut my throat...he is beating my face with all this anger and rage... violently beating me, trying to cut my throat...so much hate...I'm going to die...I'm really going to die...

He is bent on killing me...this monster from your worst nightmare...

Time seems suspended, this cant be real...it's like a dream, a bad dream...Please! Please!

I'm going to die... I'm going to die in this room tonight; I'm really going to die...

I'm caught in this small space between the closet and his bed, I keep trying to slide back away from this monster, he is constantly punching me...

Slashing at me...

I get where my back is to the wall. I think about beating on the wall and calling for help but I remember that the people who live there were leaving as we were entering Black's house and he continues to tell me to shut up...am I yelling? I don't remember...I know I'm crying, begging, pleading...

Oh God I'm going to die, I say over and over then I remember what the visiting Pastor had said earlier at church, be careful what you say...so I think ok, ok the next thought that I have is "God has not given me a spirit of fear, but of power and of love and of a sound mind" I then start begging for water, I don't know why water but I did. I keep begging and begging and he's yelling no, I ain't giving you no water I'm trying to kill you!

I need some water, I need some water, I need some water...for some reason he stopped and then handed me the water he had brought into the room earlier. I am thinking I really don't want water; I was hoping maybe he'd go out of the room and maybe I could escape...

He tried again to cut my throat, this time holding the knife to my throat and slowly cutting across, as I tense up with fear; again God I believe, did not let this knife slice my throat.

He makes a comment about the knife not cutting, He tells me to shut up again and be still, and then he grabs another knife, a steak knife that was nearby on his TV stand. He says he is going to stab me in the heart with one and cut my throat with the other.

Oh God what do I do...I don't know what to do now...

He heads towards me it seems like an eternity passes...

He gets right in front of me, hovering over me, then...all of a sudden he starts to cry, saying I said once I started, I wasn't going to stop until you was dead and I was dead...

He also says he couldn't believe he stopped. he says you know why I stopped, I don't know if I had responded to his question...I stopped because for one moment you looked just like your Mother and your Mother is so beautiful to me, she's the nicest, kindest person I've ever met, and because you look like her I can't kill you now. And just like that, all the anger and rage subsided.

Although he stopped beating me and trying to kill me, he still was holding me hostage. He says I needed to go to the hospital and that I needed a bandaid which he decided to go look for. I was thinking this man is crazy, No bandaid is going to hold my wounds together. God please get me out of here!

I asked him if I could go look in the mirror because I could feel my face swelling up and I wanted to look at my eye. He escorted me to the bathroom and gave me a washcloth that he had dampened. I looked in the mirror and I saw that my whole right side of my face was swollen and I looked at my deformed looking forearms. I'm thinking this is the results of his powerful and angry blows; this is how hard he was punching me. I looked at my eye and I could see a long red mark going down the white part of my eyeball. This is where the knife went in and was pulled back out of my eye. No gushing fluids so far…

I pat my face with the cloth. I then step back into the kitchen where he is looking in his backpack for a bandaid. I noticed that he had put our cell phones and both knifes on the kitchen counter. When he sees me he says take off your clothes I want to have sex with you. I say no I don't want too I'm scared plus you know how I feel about that. He jumps up and comes towards me saying SHUT UP you ain't in control here, I'm in control!

He starts to rip my shirt off then he says no if I do that they'll say I raped her, so instead he took the time to unbutton my shirt. I think, whether he rips my shirt off or not, he probably is going to now rape me and then kill me. I'm also thinking that he is mad at me for all the times that I said no to him pertaining to sex. I'm scared but I know I have to try to escape from this frightening man. I look at the door with all the locks secured and I think I want to try and run to the door and get out but he is so muscular and strong, he'll probably catch me plus I was thinking if I do get out that door I don't want to be running away nude! So I try to distract him from the thought he has; I say you know what I really do need that bandaid. He gets my shirt off and says you're right let me find a bandaid. He turns back to his backpack sitting on the floor and starts rummaging through it for the bandaids. I see my cell phone on the counter and I grab it and stick it in the back of my pants, tucking it in the top at the small of my back. I try to think how I can be alone so I ask him if I could go wet the washcloth he gave me again, he says yes. I head to the bathroom and I immediately look for a place to hide my phone. I decide to place it on the back of the toilet under a towel that hung over it from a rack above. Then I stepped back into the kitchen. I have to think of something else to say to get him to let me close the door; so I say all this has made my stomach upset I exclaim, I have to use the bathroom so can I close the door. He says go ahead. I'm thinking good now I can call 911 and get out of here! Just as I'm about to get the door closed, like a scene from a movie; Black burst into the bathroom. Where is your phone he says...I don't know, where did you put it? I respond. Don't play games with me where is it! I walk out of the bathroom so he won't look around for it and I head to the kitchen. He follows me, still asking where I put the phone. I say I didn't have it, he says I know I put it on the counter. Then he grabs his cell and calls mines. I pray he won't hear the gospel Song that plays as my ringtone. He doesn't then he heads to the bathroom and calls it again...he hears it ringing under the towel. He picks it up and gives me a piercing look. What was you going to do with this? I say I, I don't know, I just wanted to know where my phone was in case you start acting crazy again. I see I can't trust you. Go sit down in that chair! He yells. So I go and sit down again like an obedient little puppy. Back in the same chair where everything originated from at the beginning of this horrible night.

I used to think that if I were back in slavery time that I would have been like Harriet Tubman. I would have rebelled, fought back and helped others to escape. Harriet was a strong black woman I admired her courage and strength. I had acted out her life in a one woman show and from that had learned so much about her, yes that is how I pictured I would have been just like her. But after being beaten and almost killed, I became very submissive. What an eye opener, you never really know how you'd react under circumstances beyond your control.

Now that I am in that chair he comes in the room and sits in the same place on the end of the bed. He begins fussing angrily. Why you tell my Mother about my business! I didn't tell her anything she didn't already know I say. Shut up yes you did, he is raging on as he is putting ointment on this long gaping cut that goes across my whole right hand. He is scaring me again with all his yelling. I hope he won't start punching me in my face again because if he does I'm sure something is going to burst in my brain this time with my face being so swollen. He says I'm going to call my Mother and don't you say a word. He calls her phone and puts the phone on speakerphone; his step Father answers and says his moms asleep. He hangs up then he starts back with the "I'm gonna turn myself in after all this is over" he keeps saying that; is he going to kill me? Did he decide he just wants me dead and he's not going to kill himself now, just me? Listen I won't tell anyone about this, I'll say I got mugged, ok I promise I won't tell. Do you hear me Black, I won't tell...

He is in his own crazy thoughts as he puts the baby size bandaid on my hand wound that he is dressing. Thinking out loud he says it's probably gonna be cold in there so I'm gonna need my hoodie. Then he starts thinking of what shoes he's going to wear, wow, he's a lunatic, he's nuts, who plans what they're going to wear to jail.

So then sadly the next thing he does is raped me. During the time of his criminal sexual conduct, I lie to him to convince him that I would never leave him and that I forgave him, I say but as long as you promise that you'll never hit me again. I reiterated that I would not tell the Police, I'd go to the hospital and say I got mugged.

The whole sexual act repulsed me; it made me want to throw up! Here is this man over me, looking down at me (the light was on) seeing all the wounds he's inflicted and the blood and he's doing what he is doing. Yet I still know that I have to convince him of these things because I truly feel that when he finishes, he is still going to kill me. To my surprise, he finally believes me and starts making all these promises of changing. He says ok I'm gonna change, I won't smoke because I know you don't like that and I'm going to do this and I'm going to do that...he is going on and on with promises. Then he says and I'm gonna help you move your stuff from your old office to your new office. I but in with yes, yes I need to move my stuff, Gary and Mike will be looking for me in the morning, I'd better go... I'd say anything that would get me out of there.

He finished, then got up and laid my keys and cell phone on the bed. That was the first time I felt that I was actually going to get out of there. I knew not to shower afterwards because I had watched so many episodes of CSI which showed that you would be processed after a rape or sexual assault. That was one of my favorite shows but after being a real victim of a crime I couldn't watch anymore shows like that. I couldn't even watch any shows that had any type of violence in them without tripping or panicking.

He told me to go to the hospital and tell them someone did this to me he says they can't make you tell. I say is that what I should do, he says yes. Ok then that's what I'll do I say. He then walked me to my car, said I love you, call me when you leave the hospital. Like he didn't just try to kill me and rape me, like nothing ever happened.

I got into my car and drove right to the Police station, shaking, traumatized and upset. When I got there I couldn't even find the door to the Police station, I was so confused and disoriented, I call 911 and said I need help, someone just tried to kill me, I'm in your parking lot and I don't know where to come in. They kept trying to direct me as I drove around but I was not understanding or finding the entrance. Finally they had to send Officers out to the parking lot to get me. The Officers informed me that I needed to get to the hospital right away instead of coming in to make a report. They said they would get the details later at the hospital. They then asked me if I minded riding in the back of the Police car or did I want to wait for an ambulance. I said I didn't mind riding in the car. They drove me immediately to the hospital. The Officers were so kind; I just remember feeling safe...

At the hospital I was processed with a rape kit. They took my clothes and bagged them for evidence. I don't remember if I had shoes on. They swabbed my vaginal area and my mouth. They used a comb to collect body hair and they cut out a small section of my hair. I was also stitched up and had blood work drawn and they gave me medicines in case of STD's or infections he could have caused.

The hospital staff asked me what happened, I told them. The Officers stayed around for awhile and questioned me as well. They asked me where is he at right now, I said he is at home watching television. They told me that they were going to pick him up but they were going to tell him that it was just for questioning. They would leave and come back several times just to assure me and keep me informed as to what was going on. They knew I was so terrified that he might flee and then come after me again. At one point they told me that when they went to his apartment, he didn't answer but they could hear the TV. They went back again and he opened the door. They took him in. He lied and said we had a fight and then I asked him to have sex, and that it was the best sex ever. The last part of that statement is what rapists think because they get off on controlling their victim with fear. The Police knew he was lying. Common sense tells you that easily by the fact that he didn't have not one bruise, scratch, bite or any other defensive marks on him and what woman after being beaten, cut up, stabbed and almost killed, would say that.

The Detective also came to the hospital. He asked me to repeat my story and informed me that he would be filing the actual report and charges. I told him I was still frightened even though they arrested him because I was afraid he might escape or his family may bail him out. He told me that they were going to set his bail so high that they wouldn't be able to do that. He said they would set it at 100,000. cash and no one could pay ten percent or anything else other than the whole amount. That helped ease my mind a little. Canton Police department was excellent.

People always ask me if Black was high that day and the answer is no, he was clean and sober. Just crazy and demon possessed! But he knew what he was doing and had premeditated my murder.

CHAPTER 3

MY THOUGHTS AND ACTIONS

SHORTLY AFTER

MY THOUGHTS...............

The month of June, just after the attack on my life...I am in pain from my wounds, I struggle to make sense of what just happened. I can't look at myself in the mirror; I look like a monster to me. My family says you don't, but I say yes I do...I cry.

I battle inwardly with days of feeling overwhelming fear or days of anxiety or panic attacks.

I feel alone, even though I know that there are so many who have shown me love and support.

I think I'm going crazy because I can not control my emotions! I feel sad every day, day after day...

a week passes, I feel the emotion of anger, hmmmmm why didn't I feel that before, I ask myself.

I close my eyes I see Black attacking me...trying to kill me...I don't sleep

I think I was so terrified that I don't remember feeling the pain of what he was doing to me...did I feel it, the pain...I don't know

Everything startles me; I keep jumping out of my skin...

When I get well enough I try to drive, I get in the car and I can't, its like everything is in fast forward mode and I'm moving in extreme slow motion...too much happening, I can't drive.

I have to work hard at focusing on any type of work or other similar task, including how to spell simple words (this scares me). I just want to be back to me

I am having problems with remembering things...I can't make some of my memories come back, I try hard...I can't

I used to hear a praise or worship Song in my Spirit, always playing in the background of my mind from the moment I wake up, it is gone now, I so desperately want and need it back.....I listen for it.........I can't make it come.

I can't say the "R" word and can manage to say I survived attempted murder but I can't say and ra...I'm too ashamed and embarrassed...

It has been about three months now. My outer wounds have healed well, however inwardly I am still struggling. To others on the outside I look like I'm recovering fine, but what they don't see is the inward battle where when I'm not actively doing something and I am lets say driving alone or in the room alone I can't get those horrific thoughts of that day and its aftermath out of my mind.

I start therapy, WOW she (Chris) helps me to understand my thoughts and feelings, I'm not going crazy just healing. She explains to me what happens when we go through a trauma. She tells me my brain is still in a place of shock and is still trying to protect me. At that time, it releases extra chemicals to do this and that it is fighting against the logical side of the brain. This is why I can't control my emotions and thoughts. Anything that triggers a memory from that night, a sound, a smell, a color a visual etc. will cause my brain to react in a protective mode.

It takes me being in therapy to realize that my body is so tensed up and I'm breathing shallow...I have to practice taking deep breathes and also letting my muscles relax...it's like they are still so tense from fear.

I see the world so differently now. When I'm out, I think as someone walks past me that they will hurt me, I say to myself, in my head, Are they going to hit me, I tell myself no, it's ok, they are just walking by, you'll be ok.

A life is so, so vulnerable, it is so easy for someone to kill you...I'm terrified of men and scared of people...

Every time I get in my car I just want to take off and run away from Michigan...Chris says that's because my mind still thinks I need to escape...

I feel so sad when I think of the people who did not survive murder...it saddens me because I know what it is like to look into the eyes of the person who is trying to kill you, that is a horrific, horrific feeling...I thank God I survived but I cry for those who did not...

I used to have happy smiling eyes...now they are lifeless eyes...even when I try to smile and try to hide the pain; people can still see the sadness in my eyes that goes deep down to my soul...

I don't think a day has passed by that I don't have some kind of thought of Black or that day or my attack...this is even now after over three years have passed.

One day I wrote I wish I were dead...why, why would I say that...?

I feel so alone, so isolated in my own little crazy world...I don't think anyone can understand that, I don't even understand...

I cry often, many times I can't figure out why. No one knows the inner struggles I'm really having...

CHAPTER 4

THE AFTERMATH

PSALM 91

1 He that dwelleth in the secret place of the most High shall abide under the shadow of the Almighty.

2 I will say of the LORD, He is my refuge and my fortress: my God; in him will I trust.

3 Surely he shall deliver thee from the snare of the fowler, and from the noisome pestilence.

4 He shall cover thee with his feathers, and under his wings shalt thou trust: his truth shall be thy shield and buckler.

5 Thou shalt not be afraid for the terror by night; nor for the arrow that flieth by day;

6 Nor for the pestilence that walketh in darkness; nor for the destruction that wasteth at noonday.

7 A thousand shall fall at thy side, and ten thousand at thy right hand; but it shall not come nigh thee.

8 Only with thine eyes shalt thou behold and see the reward of the wicked.

9 Because thou hast made the LORD, which is my refuge, even the most High, thy habitation;

10 There shall no evil befall thee, neither shall any plague come nigh thy dwelling.

11 For he shall give his angels charge over thee, to keep thee in all thy ways.

12 They shall bear thee up in their hands, lest thou dash thy foot against a stone.

13 Thou shalt tread upon the lion and adder: the young lion and the dragon shalt thou trample under feet.

14 Because he hath set his love upon me, therefore will I deliver him: I will set him on high, because he hath known my name.

15 He shall call upon me, and I will answer him: I will be with him in trouble; I will deliver him, and honour him.

16 With long life will I satisfy him, and shew him my salvation.

I placed this Psalm here because so many verses blessed me. I especially clung to "He shall cover thee with his feathers, and under his wings shalt thou trust" I needed this safe place. Read each verse carefully and you will understand why I feel like it is a reflection of how God kept me, protected me and above all loved me. Thank you Lord.

When I left the hospital I drove shakily to my Sister and Mom's house. On the way I called my ex-Husband and told him what happened; we have always maintained a good friendship. I didn't call my girls or anyone else in my family because I didn't want to scare them. I decided to tell them later. When I arrived at my Mom's house, I knocked or rang the bell, I don't know which...they answered and I busted out in tears as I said Black just tried to kill me! They consoled me and took me in their home because I was in no shape to return to mine. Plus I was still terrified that Black would some how escape and come to my house and find me. Needless to say when I told my Dad and the rest of my family and friends, everyone was enraged and in shock. In fact so many people asked where he was and wanted to get him for what he'd done to me. These were good law abiding people who normally wouldn't talk of revenge. I guess when someone you love is severely attacked, you don't know what to do or how to respond when first given the news, so you may say the very first thing that comes to mind.

My oldest Daughter lived in Georgia and was the last to know because we couldn't reach her at first. When we finally did contact her, she and her friend drove up to Michigan.

Black's Mother contacted me and asked if I was ok and what happened. She said the detective called her. I told her and she said Black told her and his family a crazy story they didn't think was true. She said she was sorry for what happened and then she told me that when Black's Sister went to visit him she noticed that the jail had a list of how many people could visit each inmate. The inmates had to select five; her Brother Black had listed me as one of those people who could come visit him. His Mother said they explained to him saying that, you just tried to kill Rhonda and she is not going to come visit you!

Jumping ahead a little, his family was nice and concerned until they realized he was going to prison then their attitudes changed. His oldest Sister called me with an attitude and tried to get me to drop the charges. I told her that the state of Michigan was the one who brought charges and I would never drop the charges even if I had a say so in the matter. His Mother made a call to me also, trying to talk me out of it saying he probably was not trying to really kill me, I reminded her of the details and she backed down. His Grandmother also called one day after hearing a radio interview I had done and started fussing about her Grandson and that it was wrong for me to send him to prison. I told her she should be talking to her Grandson about the fact it was wrong for him to try to kill someone and rape them, he is to blame for him going to prison not me I told her then hung up. Everyone including my Counselor told me not to take any more calls from his family.

Back to where I was, the following Sunday was Father's day and my family, friends and church member's came to my home and packed up my things and put them in storage. On top of that in the week to come they packed my office things from both locations and placed them in two additional storage units.

Mignon, my oldest Daughter said I was coming to Georgia with her until I needed to return for the court date. Mignon drove my car because I still wasn't in condition to drive and I rode with her.

Her friend, Heather drove Mignon's car and my other Daughter Alicia rode with her. That was my first of many trips to Georgia in my trying to escape from the nightmare in Michigan. We would attend her church while I was visiting there and one day her Pastor gave me a prophetic word; he said I would be living in Georgia too, I hope he's right because I liked it there and whenever I had to return to Michigan, I would cry buckets of tears each and every time.

Speaking of court dates, the Detective on the case called me and told me that the media had gotten wind of my story and wanted to interview me and put the story on the news. I said NO I don't want my story on the news; nobody wants to be "the news". Nevertheless the media still aired the story, they told everything from what had happened, where it happened, who did it, including his picture, to how I got away. The only thing they didn't reveal was my name. It was also in all the newspapers and on the internet. People started calling me when they saw his picture to ask me was that story about me. I'd say yes and they'd say well we are going to be at court with you for support. I would immediately say no, I don't want any of my family or friends there, I would explain that I am going to have to testify about what happened and I don't want to do that in front of them. These people knew my court date before I even knew it, thanks to the media.

So many people expressed their feelings after the fact. One of my dear friends told me of a horrific story involving his ex-Wife being abducted and the horrible things that happened to her and that she was almost a victim of human trafficking too, luckily she survived but she too went through the aftermath of a terrible crime. He as her Husband also went through his own aftermath as most families do. My other friend told me that she was so afraid for me that she'd be at work worried about what if he escaped and she said she kept thinking that I've got to get out of town. She said she was so worried for me that she could not stop thinking about what I should do. After hearing what she had to say I started thinking, I wonder how this is affecting other family or friends; so I asked others to write about how they were feeling. Those are the letters I shared with you in the next chapter. Another friend told me the man she was dating showed some scary signs and she remembered some of the things I had said so she decided to get out of that relationship. She preferred to be safe than sorry.

One day while I was riding in the car with my best friend Monica, we were sharing a laugh when all of a sudden she put her finger to my head in a gun like gesture, I immediately pushed her hand away from my face and tried to laugh it off but I guess my face showed so much fear it startled her and she said I'm so sorry, I shouldn't have done that. I said it's ok. She said no it's not Romo, the nickname she calls me, your face looked so terrified. Hmm, I didn't even realize I had looked that way.

Another time another good friend and I went to a well known restaurant in an upscale community; a big fight broke out with a large group of teens. Everyone immediately ducked down in case gunfire ensued but I stood straight up and stared in that direction; frozen as she said get down. I couldn't I had to know what was going to happen, I could not be caught off guard again. The Police were called, things were contained and no gunfire transpired. Of course after the fact my behavior frightened me, that was very dangerous yet I could not alter my actions. My mind refused to let me get caught by surprise like I did that night of my attack.

My Father paid most of my car notes and insurance for me which was very nice of him. I know that it was financially hard on him. One time he was upset and said he was taking the car since he's paying on it and people keep asking him why is he riding around with a car that gives him troubles and letting his Daughter drive a newer car that he is making most of the payments on. I left the house with the car because I didn't want to hear him arguing and I didn't want him to take the car. He calmed down later and let me keep it. On another occasion my Dad came over my Sister and Mom's house to visit; they were talking and I came down from my room which I rarely did; they were conversing about snorkeling and my Dad mentioned something about being afraid. I said dad I can teach you, it's fun and I won't let anything happen to you. He said are you kidding me, you couldn't even save yourself! I was so hurt inside, I quietly faded away from the family and retreated to my room where I balled my eyes out, my Daddy even thinks it's bad I couldn't save myself, I sobbed. Shortly as some days had passed I saw my Dad again and I said daddy you made me so sad the other day. He said how, in a very concerned voice. I said when you referenced that I couldn't even save myself when Black tried to kill me. He said what! I was not talking about that. I was talking about the time you told us the funny story of when you got stuck in those high reefs in Jamaica. I would never say that to you, I love you. I hugged him tight and said oh, sorry thank you and I'm glad I talked to you about it.

Sometimes survivors are overly sensitive to what people say and we can take it the wrong way so just stay mindful of that when dealing with a survivor and make sure they have a clear understanding if it seems like they are taking the meaning of your conversation the wrong way.

I have to go back and forth to court and this is only to say we'll be coming back on another court date! The first time I saw him in court I was afraid to look at him in fact I didn't look at him for a long, long time. I had an Attorney named Luke Skywalker... yes I had the same response as you just had, "Star Wars" He was very good. Before we entered the courtroom that day, I was asked if I knew if he had any prior similar offenses. I say I don't think so. They tell me of his record that came back for offenses in Chicago and Indiana. They also share the dates with me and tell me Black said that was his Brother using his name. I tell them that is true because on the dates in question, Black was here in Michigan. I also tell them that I know his Mother had told him his Brother was using his name every time he got arrested. I could have lied and said I didn't know anything because from what I was told, if those offenses were true then he'd get a lot more time. I may have wanted him to get that extra time on top of the maximum time they told me he may receive which at that time was a whole lot, but I couldn't lie so I didn't. I knew he'd get his in the end.

When that very first court date in the Plymouth-Canton district came around and because the crime was still very fresh I was still mentally and emotionally struggling with everything. My ex-Husband Rick's Aunt Renee who I still consider my Aunt, is a victim's Advocate with her nonprofit. She is one of the people who called after hearing what happened. I had not heard from nor seen her in a long time. She was very helpful and knowledgeable about what to expect. She was one of the only people I wanted to accompany me to court. The other two people that I really needed to be there with me were Pastor Lane and Pastor Kelly. They will probably never understand or know how much I needed their presence with me. Hopefully I can convey that with my words here. I didn't know why it was so important to me that my Pastor's be there but now as I ponder it and reflect back, perhaps it was because I saw Pastor Lane as a strong, confident, protective, spiritual covering that I needed then and Pastor Kelly has this amazing God given gift to be so loving; her voice alone brings a sense of peace. Her genuine Mother instincts assure you everything is going to be alright. I felt safe with them there. They were the spiritual caring Parents I needed to hold me up in my broken state.

These three people along with the court appointed victim's Advocate were all there with me as we headed into the court and sat down. When Black was brought into the court I sat trembling with fear as Renee and Pastor Kelly put there arm around me or squeezed my hand. My body tensed up from the emotional state I was in and from their touch. When he saw Pastor Lane he dropped his head in shame. Then tried to play it off and speak to the Pastor. I didn't have to testify that day because they were having a hard time getting an Attorney to take his case. From what my Attorney and the other people that worked with my case were telling me, when several defense Attorney's read the details of our case they'd say they did not want to represent him. Then finally this female Attorney took his case. By then it was late in the day so they had to reschedule.

When I did have to testify I went up was sworn in and started telling what happened. I would not look at Black then at some point during my testimony I looked over at him, he looked very angry; I turned away very quickly. Then I decided no, I'm going to look in the face of this man who did this to me so I look back at him as I continued my testimony. He can't hurt me now; I'm safe here in court. His Attorney tries to reword what I said to see if she can trick me but I know exactly what happened so don't even try me lady! She later tells my Attorney I was very good on the stand. Afterwards I figured out why Black was griming (A harsh severe look) me so angrily when I was on the stand, he had just come to the realization that I did not lie to the Police as he told me too. It hit him as I recounted that night.

When I mentioned about what he told me when we first met about him driving fast and reckless and getting in that accident with that girl in the car, some people including the one's sitting in the little room with me at the court, started saying maybe it wasn't an accident, maybe he did it on purpose. Maybe he was trying to kill her and himself then too...I wonder now was he?

The local court hearings were just to prove there was enough evidence to go to circuit court which is where the trial would take place. Once my case went to circuit court I was given a new Attorney she was fierce, firm and mean when it came to her job. One day my Sister informed me that someone from the courts called and said Black was going to be in court that Monday and usually the courts would tell me so that I could exercise my rights to be present whenever he was seen in court. So I called to inquire if it was true and what this court date was going to be about; well she was so quick to cut me off and wouldn't even let me say things how I wanted to say them and I felt she was quite intimidating on the phone but I still tried to stand my ground and exercise my rights. This was the first time we had spoken to each other so I was taken back by her approach over the phone. When I hang up I burst into tears and said she sure is mean but I'm glad she's my Attorney because I would not want to be on the opposing side against her! She was the best at her field of expertise and the courts had specifically appointed her to my case. When we met face to face she apologized and told me that everything she does even that phone call was to prepare me for court.

One day when I attended circuit court in Detroit my newly appointed Advocate for this court district and I entered the courtroom as some other cases were in session. The guards escorted Black in and sat him over to a seating area over to the side off the Judge's bench. I could feel him staring at me, whenever we were at court I usually still did not look at him so the last time I did was when I testified. For some reason I glanced over at him and he silently mouthed the words "I'm sorry, please forgive me" several times then to my surprise I mouthed "ok" then he mouthed "I love you" and I quickly turned my head and looked at the Judge to see if she noticed him saying things. You don't say you're sorry unless you are guilty, isn't that incriminating? One of the Bailiff's saw Black trying to talk to me and mouth's to me "do you want to come over here and talk to Black?" I shake my head vigorously, no with big doe like eyes. The other Bailiff see's what is going on and walks over to that Bailiff then whispers to him; probably explaining I'm not Black's family, I'm the victim. The first Bailiff fusses at Black and tells him to stop talking to me, thankfully. My Attorney told me if he does that again get her attention. You may think he meant what he was mouthing to me but I think it was more that he thought that if he could convince me of those things that I would drop the charges and all of this court stuff would go away. Well that was not going to happen!

In the many times of going back and forth to court it was always changed to a new date but when it was finally determined that Black really was not going to take the plea, a date was finally set for trial. On this time when I arrived there where lots of people waiting in the hallway outside of the courtroom. I saw Black's Sisters and I saw people who were to be selected for Jurors for our case. I thought they don't even know that I am the victim. I got with my victim's Advocate who as I mentioned accompanied me just like she did at all the other court dates. Then I saw my Attorney, she whisked me off to this door that was next to the entrance to the courtroom. It was a tiny hallway with two benches that were just inside of the door and along the walls on both sides. It had two other side doors that led into two different courtrooms. These doors were separate from the main entrance. This little area is where they kept those who had to testify. There was an Officer seated on the opposite side, he was there for another case then the Detective for my case came in and sat down. He had a bag with evidence in it. When my Attorney came back she told me that they were going to be selecting the Jurors during that morning and that we won't actually have the trial until that afternoon. She also informed me that Black's Mother was there and she was going to subpoena her to testify. I figured that Black may have told his Mother something that was incriminating during his phone calls with her while he was in jail. I know from what Suzette, my Attorney told me, she is allowed to listen to the tapes of all the phone calls of the person she is prosecuting. That's why I think something was said that would help my case even more. I knew that my testimony and the evidence from the Detective along with his testimony were very strong but I guess that would also be the icing on the cake, so to speak. She left out again and I briefly spoke with the Detective and would hold polite conversation with others seated there. After awhile Suzette returned and said for all of us to come into the courtroom. We were seated and Black was already in the courtroom. The Judge told us that Black decided to take the plea now. Because he did, two of the five counts were dropped. She gave us the date to come back for sentencing. I think that Black finally took the plea because of the fact that his Mother was going to have to testify and I think he didn't want to put her through that. That is just my opinion, who knows what made him make that decision on that day. My Attorney later spoke at HUMS' (a nonprofit organization I started) first fundraiser. Although I felt he deserved a much longer sentence, I still appreciated her and all she did in my case, thanks, Suzette.

At a point early in my healing journey I tell the Lord that wherever he wants me to go and tell my story I will go. This came about after I had sought the Lord on what he wanted me to bring out of this tragedy.

When I was running my Mortgage company and Property Management company I had attended a Donald Trumpp seminar and had met and talked with one of the members of his staff. The staff member had asked me what I did, I told him and he told me of a guy named John who resides in New Zealand and who was trying to help people whose houses were going into foreclosure just as my company was trying to do. He put John and I in contact with each other and we communicated via email and phone. After my attack John had not heard from me in quite awhile. Once I was well enough I contacted him and told him of my plight. He said you should tell your story, start a website and tell it there and go on the radio or TV and share your story. I said no I don't want to tell my story then I remembered what I had prayed about. So I changed it to well if I tell my story I don't want my name mentioned or my face shown. He said that's fine I just think it would be good for you and others.

John actually came here from New Zealand to meet me and my family. He is a wonderfully kind man with a beautiful Wife and family. I didn't get to meet them; they were still in New Zealand but I was told by John about their concern for me and my family. His one Daughter even became long distance friends with my two younger Daughters. He will always hold a special place in my heart. And from his encouragement and my prayers I was lead to start my nonprofit and to tell my story.

I seek a name for the nonprofit, I think about what I felt or what I needed. My first thought was that I felt safe in His (God's) arms but then I thought other women might take that name the wrong way and associate it with NOT feeling safe in "his" the perpetrator's arms. Then my next thought was of what I needed, I thought about how I felt deflated and needed uplifting. Uplifting in my heart, my mind and my soul; that was it! I know many women have to feel this same way too. I came up with the acronyms for it by utilizing the four words in the title. I know you're wondering why it is HUMS instead of UHMS well simply because uhms is how most victims feel when it comes to remembering things; we have a vocabulary full of uhms! Uhm I forgot this, uhm I can't remember that etc. So we transposed the h and the u around for a much nicer sounding word. HUMS, usually when a person "hums" they are happy. I like that picture.

Monica and I drove together so that I could go get incorporated with the state of Michigan. On the way Monica came up with HUMS theme Song. You can hear it play when you visit our website. It is a spiritually inspiring and lovely Song that has a catchy beat and also blesses your spirit. We also use our theme Song as an opening for HUMS events. Thanks Monica for your God given talents, ah Monica, could you sing a Song right here? Just kidding, I always try to get her to sing, just thought I'd give it a try (smile).

My Daughter Mignon sent information via email to several television and radio shows so that I could share my story. The very first time I speak it is on the Russ Parr morning show, a national syndicated radio show. I tell his Producer that I don't want my name mentioned on the air and she says ok, she tells Russ. As soon as I get on the air, Russ says we have Rhonda Knight on the air, Rhonda tell us your story. Well so much for not having my name mention. I am ok with that now and I accepted it even then, I came to the conclusion that it was ok to use my name and to show my face.

After I spoke I felt rather sad so I didn't go to our website to see if any listeners went there, I just went home and laid down. The next day was when I finally went to the website and I was surprised to see that even though I spoke very early in the morning, around 400 people had visited our website and many left their stories on our guestbook page and in our forum. I realized that my telling my story really was helping others. I knew then without a shadow of a doubt that this is surely a part of my ministry God has ordained for me.

Jumping back a little, I also had started counseling shortly after my attack which helped a lot. My Counselor Chris tells me that the Police needs a survivor to come and speak to the public. She asked me if I felt up to it. I say yes. So I go to speak for the Police department and my Daughter Amber accompanies me. I am nervous before I get up there to speak because I had only told my story on the radio and not in person. I never really get nervous on stage because of my acting background and training and because I have ministered too. But it is different when you are telling such a personal intimate story about yourself. When I go up to speak I do it with the strength and confidence I need to convey my story and just as I am professionally trained to do, I leave nervousness behind so that I can effectively do the job I was asked here to do.

I am also asked by a Social Worker and Therapist at another facility, would I come and speak to an all men's group at a rehab facility that will consist of several perpetrators among the audience. I say yes I will. I didn't know what this would be like talking to an all male group because I didn't know how they would respond. Women are caring and compassionate when you speak before them and although I had spoken to men and women on occasion in a general audience setting, I was wondering how an all men's group would react to my story especially those perpetrators in the audience.

People started asking are you going by yourself. And I'd say yes, and they'd voice their concern so then I got a little scared. I call my best male friend's Brother who is this handsome big strong buff guy, and asked him if he'd go with me. He said yes so we went and he sat in the audience. As I spoke I told the men that at the end of my speaking I am going to challenge you. I said most abusers or assaulters are men so what are you going to do to make a difference as a man. I don't mean all men are this way but I need men to take a stand against violence along with us women in this country. Sometimes a man will listen to another man's advice faster than anyone else's. There are many ways you can make a difference; you have to take the first step which is getting involved.

As I started telling my story, these men were captivated to my surprise and they would respond with compassionate remarks just as female listeners did. I felt at ease speaking to them. At the end I opened up the floor for comments. Several men said they had experienced rape or molestation as a child and had not told anyone but they know that it is probably the cause of them being there. Many told their stories. Another told of molesting his Sister as a child and expressed how he was so ashamed that he thinks he would have killed his Sister if she had thought about telling. He said only a few years ago he had gotten counseling for this and that he had apologized to his Sister who forgave him. I told him and others listening, you see how the devil can trick you when you sin. The devil will use your shame or guilt to make you feel you have to do even more bad things. He had so much guilt and shame that he would have killed his own Sister to stop her from telling. But doing a smart thing like seeking help by getting counseling helps you deal with those issues along with asking forgiveness of the person you hurt. And of course seeking God is the number one key. I elaborated on his story more on what is going on in spiritual warfare in a way that they could hear and understand.

Another man said there was a crazy man who lived in their neighborhood for years. He said everybody knew him as this crazy but harmless dude. He said one day his little Sister was walking in the alley and this same guy came up and tried to rape her. He stated she should have known better and been on guard against this man. I said but you said everybody knew him as a "harmless" crazy dude, how would your Sister know that he was going to do something outside of his normal behavior? He said ok I see what you're saying. A lot of men or even just people in general think you can always see warning signs which is not true in some cases. Others gave their commitments to bring about change. It turned out to be a good speaking event. I go on to speak at many other places for others and eventually for HUMS when it was established.

Earlier on, one of my business friends tells me of an awesome organization called Threat Management that among other things helps female survivors of violence. I go there and I am immediately feeling like there is hope for my extreme fear of men and my fear of people. Commander Brown shows me some simple moves to protect yourself. He gives me a tour of their facility.

I start self defense training which is free to survivors. I learn how to immobilize a person in three easy moves. I learn lots of techniques that equipped me with being confident and not afraid. I tell my HUMS volunteers to come train too if they'd like and they did. I do several HUMS events utilizing Threat Management. Although I had trained with the Police department and didn't use what I learned when I was attacked; this training was somewhat different it trained you to respond automatically.

One evening as I am watching television which is something I hardly ever take time to do, a show comes on about things gone wrong in different situations. One scene was at a court when the prisoner broke away and attacked the victim and the court officials. A surge of fear hit me as I think about what if Black would have done that, he could have got me in court where I felt I was safe. It brings on another emotional crying spell. So many triggers that set off the emotions; when you least expect it you're caught off guard and swept away...

I think God is going to give me a new name, you know like He did with some people in the bible. I feel that someone is going to give me conformation that what I am feeling is true...what will it be, I'm curious and anxious because I know when He gives me a new name it will also be a new season in my life as I emerge into the fullness of my being...

After a long while, I eventually got the gospel Songs that play in my Spirit back...

I forgave Black at some point and God reminded me that it was not only my life he spared that night but it was Black's life too. Hopefully he will change for the better while in prison. Perhaps he will seek God and do God's will now and not the devil's work.

CHAPTER 5

LETTERS FROM MY FAMILY

My Mother has always been an inspiration to my life. She may not know it, but as a woman she is an exceptional example of what I hope to be. All my life I have watched my Mom work so hard for everything that she thinks is a worthy cause. From acting and using her talent to impact an audience to dressing up in a hot claustrophobic apple costume to help young children. She's been a foster Mom to children and even an adoptive Mother to not just Kayla and Jasmyn but a host of my friends. And in a day in age when Mothers are a dime a dozen that means the world to many. You won't find a more loyal friend a more devout Christian or a more accepting woman than in my Mom. Is it any wonder that I want to be like her?

That's why when Charles Blue violently tried to take my Mother's life I drove over 750 miles from Atlanta, Georgia to be with her. Of all the obstacles and bumps in the road I know my Mom has seen, this has been the hardest for her to overcome. And rightfully so. All the strength and power my Mom has been know to exert was sucked from her. The normally confident and soundness that, in our family relative or not, she has become known for was taken from her that night Charles tried to kill her. I'm more angry at him for that then the actual fact that he abused her, I love my Mom and all I could think about for the longest time was how could I bury my Mother. I wasn't ready. Even now as I talk with her from time to time I notice a sadness in her voice that I have never heard. As she tries to put her life back together I know that Mama will soon emerge stronger and more confident then the one Charles tried to destroy, and for that I continue to send up praises to God. For the testimony has been said and our victory is in her living.

As for the man that thought he could take my Mother from her five loving Daughters, her four Sisters, one Brother, four Grandsons, three Nieces, six Nephews, Aunts, Uncles, Cousins, Friends, and other people's lives she's touched in her forty-something years in this earth as a Daughter to God, I say HA! Nice try, all you've done is make us closer, and stronger to face the devil everyday!

Mignon Williams, 1st born

Two letters from Amber

The Incident

You know you hear about incidents like these on the news or on a movie. So when it happens to you, you put yourself in a disbelief in a state of mind that this is not real. My Mother could have died about a month ago. DIED...I am angry right now you would never imagine your Mother dead because of a selfish evil controlling man. When I say controlling I mean this man was in control of my Mother's destiny, but do you know who is better than man, God. It wasn't in his plan for my Mother to die that night, but from here on out for her to touch the souls of everyone who ever thought they knew a person and what they were capable of. My Mother was someone you would never see this happening to, she has always been the strength of our family, she's always been a leader and a teacher. She is smart, would never think someone could ever cross her. My Mother has five Daughters Mignon, Amber, Alicia, Jasmyn and Kayla. She has also been a foster Mom to about six children; she has also taken half of these foster kids along with us to Mexico and several other small trips. She is a woman with a beautiful spirit and a woman of God, who hates to see people sad no matter who it is if she sees someone hurt she would do just about anything to see them smile. My Mother did not deserve for this to happen to her, especially not over the end of a friendship. Sure breakups are hard sometimes but who has the right to control a person's fate by willing to kill them if they didn't stay friends with you. This letter is supposed to be about my feelings about this incident, and I feel sad, angry, guilty, scared, and well just hurt. I am sad because I don't know how it feels to lose a parent but I could have felt it. I am angry because I thought I knew the person who did this; after all I kind of hooked them up with each other. I am guilty because if my Mom would have died that night I wouldn't be able to tell you the last time I talked to her. I am scared because I don't know if my Mom would ever be back to how she used to be. I am hurt because my Mother is hurt and this is the incident that has changed our lives.

Amber Fields, Second Daughter

Second letter…

My name is Amber and I am the second oldest Daughter to Rhonda Knight. When my Mother asked me to write a letter about how I feel about what happened, it never occurred to me that this letter would help me heal also. You see a few weeks ago I could have lost my Mother, my friend, my strength, my guidance, my hero, my everything. You see my Mother's life was in the palm of this strangers hand and when I say stranger I mean a man I thought I knew but it is obvious I did not. You see if it wasn't for me my Mom would have never known this man, I pretty much set them up together. So yes you could imagine the pain I am going through. You know when you are used to seeing a strong, independent, kind, loving and well spoken woman who always has her head up high, it frightens you to see that person in any other way. My Mother was the strength of our family, no matter what the situation was she taught us to have faith and don't worry about anything, "everything will be ok" she would always say. That's why it is so sad to see her in this way. She went from that motivational person to this sad and scared woman, who would've been dead right now. My Mother did not deserve to die that night and that's why she is here today to pass her story on and help others in the same situation. I am thankful today and I will be for the rest of my life because I still have my Mommy!

Second Oldest, Amber Fields

Everybody at some point of their life says, "My Moms the best!" and I couldn't agree more, my Mom is the best; she can do anything and everything she puts her mind too. She's the best role model a Daughter could ever have, a great Mom, and a woman of God! Everyone who encounters my Mother adores her; she's always full of energy and happiness. I rarely see my Mother cry, she tries to make the best out of bad situations. It has been three and a half years since this tragedy has happened to my Mother. I tend to block bad situations in my life and forget it ever happened, but this incident repeats itself every year. And every year my Mom takes it the hardest, taking days off to be alone whether it's spending the night in a hotel or taking a vacation away from reality. Let me just say that I always hated seeing my Mom with men I'd rather her be alone or back with my Father which both never happens. But of course who would want to live their life alone without a soul mate? Maybe that's what she was looking for, but I always felt she was better off without one. Is that selfish on my part or what?! Soon after my Stepfather was out of the picture from her second marriage I was relieved and happy. Happy that I had my Mother back, I'd be lying if I said he didn't change her. Yea she became more spiritual with God but my Mother always had God in her life this man just took it to the extreme. My Mother is very open-minded, never judging a person, but when she met "BLACK" I just saw him as another loser my Mother would be better off without but still held a smile and pretended to like him for my Mom. I was living in Toledo, Ohio when this tragedy occurred, about an hour away from home. I was so caught up in my lifestyle I barely had time to talk with fam, I actually didn't realize what happened until after the incident when my Father called me a day or two later to tell me my Mother almost died. That's when my life got turned upside down, everything came to a stop and I just had to speak to my Mother and hear her voice for myself, to know that she was okay but of course she was far from it. I had to go home after what she told me, I wanted to kill him myself! It's just a surreal feeling to know that your Mother could have been taken from you, that she had experienced something you only see in movies or hear about on the news about somebody else. I praise God that he spared my Mother, I don't know how I would live my life without her. My unborn child could have grown up without a Grandmother but instead God had shown his mercy on a woman of love, courage, wisdom and faith and for that I can't stop praising Him it just shows how much of an awesome God he really is.

Third Oldest, Alicia Knight

The incident not only changed my Mom's life but also mine, because what happened to her was something that no one saw coming or ever expected. It is unfortunate how you can live your life each day thinking you know a person but in reality you have no idea what they're capable of. Since the incident my Mom has been having a hard time getting her life back together and I can't help but to wonder if my Mom will ever heal.

I feel sad but at the same time angry because my Mom should not be going through this with everyone knowing that she is a very sweet person. I can't ever forgive him.

Fourth Oldest, Jasmyn Knight

What I feel about my Mom I feel sad because what happened to her, but I hope she get better but it was a sad day that day but we are hoping that she gets well. It was hard for my Mom to recover and she was always sad but we all prayed for her to get better and she got better in a week. What had happened it was mean to do but she did not deserve this, she is a nice lady no one should do that to people or my Mom it is a horrible thing… this is the sad story.

Youngest, Kayla Knight

Hi, my name is Connie Blackmon I am the Mother of Rhonda Knight who is my 2nd oldest Daughter.

Rhonda is a very outgoing person who has and still does various jobs and tasks, she is on the minister's board at her church, she has also worked as Branch Manager for a Mortgage co. She has been in many plays, has written plays, directed plays, has been a Lighting Tech. and worked as an extra in movies.

Rhonda has met such stars as:

Keanu Reeves, Ving Rhames, Jennifer Lopez, George Clooney, Danny Devito, and many others.

She has also been a foster Mom to five different children, two of which she adopted and is now their Mom. Rhonda is Mother to five Daughters (two adopted) and Grandma to four Grandsons.

She has always been a person who loves people and would help anyone that needed help if she was able too.

She is a person who loves the Lord and talks of His goodness. She has always been a cheerful, loving and affectionate person to everyone that she meets. I thank God for sparing her life she has always told people that she is my favorite Daughter. ☺ I just don't like that she looks sad at times now, but I know that time will change all of that.

Mother, Connie Blackmon

9-18-07

It was a week before Father's day, I was happy and having lunch with my lady friend at a restaurant when I received a call from my youngest Daughter LaShawn. I could not believe what I was hearing on my cell phone. TEAR'S began streaming down my face in public and I could not eat. "Daddy, brace yourself...Charles Blue said he loved Rhonda too much to live without her, so he said he was going to kill her and then himself!" "So, he began stabbing her and one of the stab wounds was in her left eye." Daddy stop crying and praise the Lord in Jesus name that you still have a Daughter!!

I was so sad that day, but I was so happy on Father's Day 2007 because, by the grace of God I still have my Daughter alive and in my life. Thank you Jesus this is one of the greatest blessings that you have ever given to me!

My second Daughter Rhonda always says, she is my "favorite Daughter," let it be known-she is not, I have three, Karmen, Rhonda and LaShawn and their Sister Tori and their Brother Michael, and I love them all equally.

However, many people say Rhonda takes after me. Because she has many talents (like myself), and she is good at all of them (like myself). She likes helping people and spreading the word of God. She has made many more accomplishments then I have. And she says, "I sometimes take after you, mostly I always follow the path that the Lord leads me in Jesus name. If that mean's change my mind and try something new, so be it". Sometimes the Lord will show us a blessing from our darkest hours. In Rhonda's case, the Lord has shown her how to start a fundraiser to help others who have been through similar experiences "like hers."

Sincerely,

Father, George E. Robinson

Website Guestbook comments...

September 28th 2007

You are constantly on my mind and heart. I shall pray every day for you. We know that with our HOLY FATHER, all things are possible. We also know that, He will never give us so much we are unable to bear. Then we also know that, to whom much is given, much is required. All these things have been handed to you. You have been given your life. The life that could have been taken away in an instance. However, OUR FATHER, saw fit to continue to use your presence here on earth, for His glory. Let us continue to put God first. Remembering whose we are, and why we are His. May Jehovah continue to orchestrate this heavenly endeavor that He has put in your hands to take care of.

Third oldest Sister, LaShawn Robinson

November 26th 2007

I AM VERY UPSET ABOUT WHAT HAPPEN TO YOU RHONDA IT HURTS THAT I WAS'NT THERE TO SAVE MY BABY SISTER BUT GOD SAVED YOU; HE WRAPPED HIS ARMS AROUND YOU AND PUT HIS GLORIOUS SHIELD OF PROTECTION AROUND YOU AND WITHIN YOU SO THAT THE WOUNDS DID NOT KILL YOU; BUT YEA IT MADE YOU STRONGER I CRIED WHEN MOM TOLD ME WE HAD A CRISIS AND WHAT HAD HAPPEN TO YOU. AND I'M SAD INSIDE NOW; FOR WHAT YOU HAD TO GO THROUGH; BUT GOD NEEDED A SPOKESWOMAN AND HE DESIGNATED YOU TO HELP MILLIONS OF BATTERED AND ABUSED WOMEN; YOU ARE TRULY BLESSED MAY GOD CONTINUOUSLY PROTECT MY SISTER ROCKY AND ALL MY FAMILY AND MYSELF MAY GOD WRAP SHIELD AND GUIDE US ALL INCLUDING THIS ONLINE FAMILY ALL THAT TUNE IN TO THIS WEB SITE. I LOVE YOU, YOUR SISTER KARMEN. LOVE YOU MOM YOUR OLDEST DAUGHTER KARMEN AND I LOVE ALL YE THAT READ THIS IN JESHUAH (JESUS) NAME PEACE SALEM AMEN

Oldest Sister, Karmen Robinson

I LOVE YOU. Grandma keep rocking on. And one day H.U.M.S. might be global. You are really sweet and nice and fun. ps from your first born Grandson Eric.

Oldest Grandson, Eric

I'm proud of you and you are the best Grandma I ever had. I will do anything I can for you. So you call me anytime. I will listen to you and GOD BLESS YOU

Twin Grandson, Dionte`

You are the best Grandmother ever. You are helpful. AND NICE. And pretty. AND SMART. I HOPE YOU HAVE A NICE DAY. YOU HAVE A NICE SMILE. GOD BLESS YOU.

Twin Grandson, Deondre`

October 11th 2007

Mom I am soooo proud of you for starting this website and reading the women you've touched by being honest and open with this horrible incident is the best thing you could have done. I hope that no one has to go through what you went through but if they do or have I know that hums will give them hope. I love you and keep up the great work!

Mignon

September 22nd, November 29th/30th 2007

A poem for you: You took from me something that you can't give back I trusted you and gave you all my respect You stood over me with the soul you lack For now I know it was my life you'd select You thought you could destroy me But undefeated I stand You thought that we would always be But that wasn't in Gods plan For I am now stronger than you've ever been I am a survivor and no I am not alone Behind me are hundreds of beautiful women And together we can move on.

Mom I am so proud to have a Mommy as strong as you and I am so happy that you are on this journey to recovery and I want you to know I love you and I am so thankful that God kept you, not only for me but for so many other survivors. I think about you every day and I thank God for you still being a part of my life. I am excited to see the blessings that God has in store for H.U.M.S. Love you forever and always, your second born Amber.

Just wanted to let you know this is a very inspirational website and I look forward to the growth of H.U.M.S. because I know it will be a successful program that will not only help me but thousands of women to come. Thank you and good luck!!

Amber

September 25th, 2007

Mom I am so proud of the cause that you are doing for woman in situations similar to yours, you were always a strong person to me and I know that no matter what, if you put your mind into something with Christ by your side, anything is possible. You have my support 100%. I love you Mommy…be blessed!

Alicia

Please visit H.U.M.S. website and read the many stories of women and some men who shared their heartfelt comments. If you would like to share your story or comment on our website, please feel free to do so as well.

www.h-u-m-s.org Go to the guestbook page and the forum page. Please sign our guestbook while you're there too. Thank you.

By the way, "Let it be known" that I AM my Dad's favorite Daughter, he is in such denial!!!

CHAPTER 6

I FIND THAT I CANNOT

SAY THE "R" WORD

THE EFFECTS OF SEXUAL ASSAULT...

I manage to be able to tell some close family or friends that I survived attempted murder but I find that I can't say and...rrrape. I really literally could not even say the "R" word (rape). It was so difficult for me to say it, so often times I wouldn't say anything about it. I feel so humiliated, so embarrassed, so ashamed so yucky and disgusted. Even though I know that I was not to blame for what happened to me I could not help but to feel this way.

I still never talk about what exactly happened during that time. If you noticed in chapter two, I didn't give a count for count detail on the things that happened during this portion of the assault. The only time I went into detail was at the hospital, for the Police and detective and when I had to testify in the regular court before it went to Circuit court. No other times do I discuss this. Why?

One of the many other effects of that sexual assault was that I continued to wear the dark glasses my Dad had bought for me to hide the injuries to my eyes. I wore them well beyond the healing time for my eyes...the reason for this is because I thought that if anyone looked into my eyes, they would be able to see everything he had done to me that night. I really thought I could hide behind those glasses, my super hero glasses "able to hide all bad things".

Deep down inside is a hurt and an emotional disturbance that is not easily gotten rid of. It is always there, sometimes lying dormant waiting to come back out in a flood of uncontrollable emotions and actions.

Right after it happened when people like my loved ones or friends or Advocates would come up to me and put their arm around me or hug me or touch me in any innocent way, my inward body would cringe and outwardly I would tense up. I did not want anyone to touch me but I never told them that. I did not want to be rude when I knew that they were just trying to show me love and support. This went on for a long time.

The only men I felt I could trust at that time were my Father, my ex-Husband Rick and my Pastor. I think I am never going to be able to have a normal relationship with anyone. I say I never ever want anyone to try to kiss me or hug me or even think about being intimate with me. This comforts me in a safety kind of way but saddens me in other ways. It makes me not me, the huggy, kissy affectionate type of person I normally am.

When I start group therapy I find out that I was not the only woman who could not say the "R" word. Every woman in that group said the same thing! We developed a tightly knitted relationship among most of us that has lasted even until this day. I consider them valuable friendships that will last even if we only get to speak to each other once or twice yearly. We all have a respect, appreciation and admiration for Chris our Therapist, (technically Counselor) as well and will always be forever grateful to her for her kindness, wisdom and support. It is sad that we had to meet under those kinds of circumstances but I'm glad we all met.

When I learned some new technique in my self defense training I would share it with my group. Then I asked if it would be alright for the group to go to training classes and most agreed they wanted too. Going to those classes were so empowering for us. Oddly we felt like we could have some control in our lives again.

One time in class there was a fairly large male member of the training staff who had to do a move with me where he simply had to swing on me as I walked in forward towards him to do my protective moves. Well I kept ducking when he would swing and I could not make myself do the move I was trained to do. Well that just broke my spirits! A deep hidden fear kept popping up which I thought I had over came. I started crying as I realized that as much as I had learned and as much as the training gave me my confidence back, there were still some triggers that could set me back. I had worked with many of the trainers and they were all well built buff guys but for some reason this guy or the way the move was orchestrated set off something that must have been reminiscent of my attack or attacker. Nevertheless I still kept training and as many of my classmates said, replaying the moves over and over in our heads to make sure no one would ever take advantage of us again!

I try dating in 2009 I go out a couple of times with a nice man I met and on one date this guy tries to kiss me, not forcibly or anything, just a kiss, I freak out and get all panicky and yes start to cry. He consoles me; I explain that I guess I am still experiencing the effects of my ordeal. He is understanding; I decide to not date for awhile. When I do date again it's just dinner here or there nothing to allow anyone to get too close.

As I do my speaking engagements, many women confide in me that they have either been a victim of assault or abuse or of rape. So many of them tell me that they have never told anyone and that they still won't tell anyone other than them confiding in me. This is thousands of women I have spoken in front of and hundreds I have spoken too and out of that number, only one said she had not experienced any type of assault or abuse. That's good but just one woman out of hundreds that is sad but true. Wake up we need to come together and make real change in this world.

Several people in my family have experienced child molestation and deal with the effects of that in their adult life. A couple has experienced rape and they too have issues resulting from the unfortunate ignorance of their perpetrator. Only recently someone near and dear to me shared that she and her Sister were molested as children by their great Uncle and that she still sometimes has nightmares. She said when she spoke to her elderly Aunt, her Mother's Sister, the Aunt said that same man tried to bother her and her Sisters too when they were little. The Aunt said not just him but the step Grandfather was a perpetrator too. This happens in a lot of families, sometimes you may even hear rumors of it in your family but most of the time it's ignored or played down. More so in the past but it is still somewhat that way in these days.

A male friend shared a tear filled moment with me sadly expressing that he was molested and raped as a child. He told me that one other person and I are the only people he's ever told this too. If females have so much difficulty talking to someone about it and dealing with it and living with it, can you imagine how hard it must be for male survivors?

If I had a magic wand that I could wave and go back in time, I would protect all of them and make sure the…ok right here so many curse words come to mind that I wish I could use but maybe that would not be appropriate on my part so I'll stick with perpetrator would never ever hurt anyone else. Other thoughts pop in my head of ways I would hurt them for hurting those I love. People like me who have to live with what another's selfish motives has done to us. That…ok, ok don't curse…that man goes on with his life leaving behind a broken person who has to deal with flashbacks, nightmares, fears, insecurities, trust issues, lack of feeling safe or strange behaviors in their adult life like making sure the shower curtain stays open because her attacker hid behind it and would wait until she came into the bathroom or not wanting the bedroom door closed and only realizing why when she was in her late sixties as it was told to me by one of my volunteers, it was because she realized that her Father would come into her room, close the door and molest her. One young lady at one of the rally's I spoke at, said it like this; one moment it would be ok for her boyfriend to touch here and then the next time she'd trip(act crazy, freak out etc.) and it would not be ok. She expressed how hard it is to be in a relationship when your partner thinks you are bipolar or have some other mental illness. She's right that's how you feel, you never know when a trigger may make you trip out.

I included this as a separate chapter in my book because I hope that those of you who are in a relationship with a survivor, male or female, will have a better understanding of your partner and learn to be more compassionate to her/him. Go to counseling with your partner, read up on the subject of what he or she went through. Help them learn techniques from professionals or from survivors who have developed ways that effectively work to help the survivor cope. Remember even with your support and all of the other things suggested, she or he may still have some bad days. Be patient and stay prayerful.

I also want Parents to be educated to the fact that we all need to watch our children more carefully. So what if people call you an over protective Parent, I'm sure you'd rather be called a name than have to have your child deal with the issues you hear about in this book. Talk to your children; develop a trusting relationship where they feel they can talk to you about anything. I thought I had established that with my own girls and yet somehow they waited before telling me of some things they had experienced. I know I did the right thing in talking to them from a very young age but children still get afraid. Eventually my girls told me but I wish it would have been sooner so that they would not have had to endure anything. My other Daughter had to unfortunately experience attempted date rape and now deals with the issues of that. Thankfully she told me the truth within a twenty four hour time period so that we could get to the hospital and have evidence gathered in a rape kit for the Police.

So I say talk, talk and talk some more, not beating them up with the subject but assuring them that you are there for them and by educating them as to what is wrong or inappropriate behavior for an adult to do to a child or teenager. Develop a lasting trusting relationship with your child. If you think it probably won't happen to your child, then I hope you are right but keep these statistics in mind; one in every four girls are molested and one out of every six boys are molested. Don't be blind and in denial of the truth of what is really happening in our country. Protect your children!

Here is an excerpt from HUMS' forum, written by a woman who uses the name: **Stronger than you**

I am stronger now...

Here I am now a woman, at age 22; I am finally able to say that after years of trying to discover who I am in result of being molested at a very tender and young age. Age 13 is when most young ladies began to develop into beautiful women for me I was forced to grow up too fast. I was molested for about two years by an older relative, to make matters worst he also bother my younger Sister. I have had to sacrifice myself sometimes to protect my Sister and also fight with this man in order to keep him out of the shower when we would be in the bathroom getting ready for school. This person took everything away from me as a young lady but now I stand a young woman, who is able to fight back by sharing along with others her story and together we will reach thousands of other women and we will teach others to come, how to be strong, because we are survivors now not victims any more.

FACT: Every two minutes, someone in the U.S. is sexually assaulted.

What is sexual assault?

Georgia Network to End Sexual Assault's (GNESA) and others combined Definition of Sexual Assault is as follows: "Sexual assault and abuse is any type of sexual activity that is against another person's will or that you do not agree to including:

- ➤ rape

- ➤ attempted rape

- ➤ child molestation

- inappropriate touching
- vaginal, anal, or oral penetration
- sexual intercourse that you say no to
- sodomy/aggravated sodomy
- fondling
- sexual harassment
- indecent exposure
- stalking
- peeping toms
- sexual battery

Sexual assault can be verbal, visual, or anything that forces a person to join in unwanted sexual contact or attention. Examples of this are voyeurism (when someone watches private sexual acts), exhibitionism (when someone exposes him/herself in public), incest (sexual contact between family members), and sexual harassment. It can happen in different situations, by a stranger in an isolated place, on a date, or in the home by someone you know.

What is rape?

GNESA's definition is "Rape is an act of violence in which sex is used as a weapon. Rape occurs when a person engages in sexual intercourse by forcible compulsion or with someone who is incapable of consent."

Facts about rape

- Rape is an act of violence, power, and control.
- Rape is motivated primarily out of anger and/or a need to feel powerful by controlling, dominating, or humiliating the victim.
- Survivors are not responsible for causing their assaults; only offenders are to be blamed for sexual assault and rape.

- Anyone can be sexually assaulted. Studies show that victims include infants to people in their eighties, people of color, immigrant and refugees, lesbians/gays, people with disabilities, and persons from every racial, ethnic, religious, economic and social background.
- No one asks to be sexually assaulted. Nor does anyone's behavior justify or excuse the crime. People have a right to be safe from a sexual violation at anytime, any place, and under any circumstances. The offender, not the victim, must be held responsible for this crime.
- If anyone forces or coerces you to have sex against your will it is rape. Even if the perpetrator is your Husband or partner.
- Familiar people and "safe" places and times are often more dangerous. A person is less likely to identify a friend, acquaintance or date as a potential rapist. As many as 80% of all sexual assaults are committed by someone the victim knows. Over 50% of all sexual assaults occur in the home and as many sexual assaults occur during the daytime as happen at night.
- It is currently estimated that one out of ten men are victims of adult sexual assault and one out of six are sexually abused as children.
- Numerous studies of convicted rapists have revealed that men have various motives for raping women, yet none of the studies has shown sexual gratification as a primary motive. The reasons given most often by rapists are power, domination, revenge, and humiliation. Rape is an act of aggression and violence accomplished through sexual means.
- The victim's past sexual history has no bearing on whether or not she was raped. Even if she has had sexual relations with the rapist before, if she was forced to have sex with him against her consent its still rape.
- If a man forces a woman to have sex, rape has occurred, whether or not she fights back.
- Though many cultures believe this to be true, there is no shame in being raped just as there is no shame in being the victim of any other type of violence, like being mugged. It is the perpetrator of this violence that deserves punishment not the victim.

Rape is a common form of sexual assault. It is committed in many situations; on a date, by a friend or an acquaintance, or when you think you are alone. Educate yourself on "date rape" drugs. They can be slipped into a drink when a victim is not looking. *Never* leave your drink unattended no matter where you are. Try to always be aware of your surroundings. Date rape drugs make a person unable to resist assault and can cause memory loss so the victim doesn't know what happened. Take steps right away if you've been sexually assaulted.

What to do if you've been sexually assaulted...

Get away from the attacker to a safe place as fast as you can. Then call 911 or the Police.

Call a friend or family member you trust. You also can call a crisis center or a hotline to talk with a Counselor.

One hotline is the **National Sexual Assault Hotline at 800-656-HOPE (4673)**

Feelings of shame, guilt, fear, and shock are normal. It is important to get counseling from a trusted professional.

Do not wash, comb, or clean any part of your body. Do not change clothes if possible, so the hospital staff can collect evidence. Do not touch or change anything at the scene of the assault.

Go to your nearest hospital emergency room as soon as possible. You or the hospital staff can call the Police from the emergency room to file a report. Ask the hospital staff about possible support groups you can attend right away.

I still cringe inside every time I say rape but I force myself to use the word because of my work...

CHAPTER 7

MY LETTER TO THE COURT

My speech at the sentencing on October 11th 2007

I wrote it in all caps then and copied and pasted it here just as it was written.

ON JUNE 11th, YOU TRIED TO MURDER ME, YOU DECIDED BECAUSE YOU WERE NOT HAPPY WITH YOUR LIFE YOU WANTED TO KILL YOURSELF BUT BECAUSE I CHOSE TO END OUR FRIENDSHIP, YOU SELFISHLY DECIDED YOU WOULD TAKE MY LIFE AS WELL, WITHOUT THOUGHT OF ME OR MY FIVE DAUGHTERS WHO'D BE LOSING A MOTHER OR MY FOUR GRANDSONS WHO I WOULD NEVER GET TO SEE GROWUP OR WHAT SUCH A TRAGEDY WOULD DO TO MY MOTHER WHOM YOU SAID YOU LOVED & MY FATHER WHO ALMOST HAD ANOTHER HEART ATTACK WHEN THIS HAPPENED AND MY OTHER FAMILY MEMBERS. ALTHOUGH MY LIFE WAS NOT PRECIOUS TO YOU, IT IS TO ME AND MY LOVE ONES, AND GOD CHOSE FOR ME NOT TO DIE THAT NIGHT WHEN YOU KEPT TRYING TO SLIT MY THROAT, BEAT MY FACE IN AND KILL ME, NOT YOU, IF YOU WOULD HAVE HAD YOUR WAY I'D BE DEAD RIGHT NOW! YOU SEE EVENTHOUGH I DIDN'T PHYSICALLY DIE THAT NIGHT, TO ME I DID DIE. YOU KILLED MY SPIRIT; YOU HAVE TOTALLY ROBBED ME OF MY LIFE AS I KNEW IT AND SO MANY OTHER THINGS. I CANNOT EVEN FIND RHONDA, SHE DIED THAT NIGHT, I DON'T EVEN KNOW WHO I AM. I MAY LOOK OK ON THE OUTSIDE BUT I AM STILL MENTALLY AND EMOTIONALLY SUFFERING AND I'M TOLD BY MY THERAPIST THAT IT COULD

TAKE A LONG WHILE BEFORE I TOTALLY RECOVER. AND YOU'VE SET IN THIS COURT ON SEVERAL OCCASSIONS AND THE JUDGE HAS TOLD YOU HOW SERIOUS WHAT YOU DID IS, YET I DON'T THINK THAT YOU HAVE ANY REMORSE AT ALL OR THAT YOU REALLY LISTENED TO WHAT JUDGE FRESARD WAS SAYING TO YOU, BECAUSE YOU'D SIT IN THIS COURTROOM AND SILENTLY MOUTH TO ME I LOVE YOU, HOW COULD YOU EVER LET THOSE WORDS COME OUT OF YOUR MOUTH WHEN THAT NIGHT YOU DECIDED TO RAPE ME RIGHT AFTER JUST TRYING TO KILL ME. YOU WERE ON TOP OF ME LOOKING DOWN AT MY FACE WITH THE LIGHT ON, LOOKING AT MY FACE WHICH WAS DEFORMED LOOKING FROM ALL THE PUNCHES YOU INFLICTED WITH ALL THE ANGER & RAGE YOU FELT AND THEN I FELT WITH THE NON STOP BLOWS TO MY FACE, AND LOOKING AT THE STAB WOUND IN MY EYE, CUTS ACROSS MY THROAT, THE OTHER KNIFE WOUNDS ON MY ARMS AND HAND. LOOKING AT ALL THIS YOU'D JUST DID TO ME AND FORCING ME TO HAVE SEX WHEN I DIDN'T WANT TOO AND TO DO OTHER THINGS TO YOU THAT I DIDN'T WANT TOO. I WAS FEELING REPULSED BY THE WHOLE THING AND WANTING TO JUST THROW UP! AND FOR YOU TO SIT HERE IN COURT AND MOUTH I LOVE YOU, THAT'S WHAT LOVE IS TO YOU? WELL THEN I PRAY THAT YOU WILL NEVER EVER HAVE THE CHANCE TO LOVE ANOTHER WOMEN LIKE YOU LOVED ME, AND THAT THIS COURT AND OUR JUDICIAL SYSTEM WILL NOT ALLOW YOU TOO. I PERSONALLY THINK MY LIFE AND ALL THAT I SUFFERED IS WORTH MORE THEN YOU SERVING 15 YEARS, BUT I HOPE & PRAY THAT AS YOU SIT THERE IN PRISON, THAT YOU WILL REFLECT ON WHAT YOU DID AND HOW TRULY, TRULY SELFISH YOU WERE AND THE IMPACT IT HAS CAUSED IN NOT ONLY MY LIFE, BUT MY FAMILY'S LIFE AND YOUR OWN FAMILY'S LIFE AND YOUR MOTHER'S LIFE WHOM YOU SAY YOU LOVE DEARLY.

CHAPTER 8

FROM WHAT I THOUGHT WAS A SAFE HOME

TO A SAFEHOUSE

PSALM 27:7-10

7 Hear, O LORD, when I cry with my voice: have mercy also upon me, and answer me.

8 When thou saidst, Seek ye my face; my heart said unto thee, Thy face, LORD, will I seek.

9 Hide not thy face far from me; put not thy servant away in anger: thou hast been my help; leave me not, neither forsake me, O God of my salvation.

10 When my father and my mother forsake me, then the LORD will take me up.

Several months have passed by and I still reside at my Sister and Mother's home. I spend most of the time in my room when I am there. The room I'm in belongs to my teenaged Nephew. The girls sleep in my Mom's room. My Sister's two younger boys who are around three and four years old sleep in her room and the oldest of my Sister's three boys sleeps in his Brother's room since I am in his room.

I am at the house unless I'm out at church, speaking, working with HUMS or doing self defense training.

One day my Mother hands me this letter from my Sister. I take it upstairs to read it. I am hurt from what I am reading. My Sister basically tells me that I have to leave because my Nephew wants his room back. Really, wow my own Sister would say that to me and my Mother who knew what the letter entailed would hand it to me; my flesh and blood.

My Nephew was in a room privately all to himself. He is a teenager. If someone tried to murder my Sister and she came to my house I would let her stay as long as she needed too. That's my Sister, I love her and if one of my kids said something like that I would tell them, your Aunt almost got killed, don't be selfish, you're in a room to yourself already, I'm going to let her stay as long as she wants and needs to stay, I love her and if you got a problem with that then you may need a spanking!

I am at this point, I'm still in the early stages of healing, no where near wanting to brave everything on my own. I felt safe there with my family, but I left at her request.

I talked to my resources about needing a safehouse for me and the girls to temporarily come too. Commander Brown just so happen to be the one who had a place available. It is in Detroit in a run down bad neighborhood. It is well camouflaged in the midst of the area. It is a loft hidden in an old abandoned looking warehouse type building. It sits behind a liquor store and you have to enter into the parking spaces through a garage door that is in the alley. Right across from this door is an abandoned house where crack heads, neighborhood drunks or vagabonds would sometimes be hanging out there in the backyard which faced the alley. The same types of people would be in the stores' parking lot too. The parking lot of the store and alley you had to drive through was riddled with broken glass. Once you entered the garage you'd see several cars parked in there. It had seven lofts I think. Only the loft I stayed in was a safehouse, the others were occupied by regular residents. Some entrance doors were right off the parking area others were through this doorway and up the stairs. Ours was off the parking area. When you enter in you are amazed to see a very large loft uniquely made.

If it would have been in another area and in another building structure it would have been a very nice loft to live in.

I am so deeply hurt by what my family did that when I left I decided not to tell anyone where we were staying and I was not speaking to them either. If they didn't care about our well being so be it. I became more depressed and cried often usually when I was in my room alone so that the girls wouldn't see me. My Dad called me and I asked him did he know that they were planning to do what they did. He said they mentioned it to him and I said that was so mean, I would never do that to anyone in my family. We talked for awhile and he consoled me. It hurt me what my Sister did but to think that my Mom was involved too made me even sadder.

The girls, Snow and I stay there for a month or two. I sleep in the upper room of the loft; it is at the top of the stairs and is the only room that is up. The girls sleep in a room on the lower level. I hear them scream about seeing centipedes just about every day and brave Kayla would kill them. I don't see any in my room but because it is an old building it has a lot of them. The girls and I do not like bugs!! However we have to endure because it is where we have to stay for now. I have to tell Jasmyn and Kayla to pay attention to their surroundings and remember everything Threat Management taught them in self defense training while they take Snow to the alley to do his business, I would stand in the doorway and watch them as one would watch the other and the other would survey their surroundings. They have always lived in the suburbs from a very early age and had no intercity living experience since being adopted at a young age. I never lived in Detroit either but had more knowledge of how to behave in certain types of situations. I also have to drive them back to the city of Romulus to school. That is about thirty minutes away on the expressway and I did the trip back and forth in the morning and then again in the afternoon. One morning as we were heading out for them to go to school, we did what we normally do and that is me and one of the girls would get in the car then I would pull the car out of the garage into the alley and my other Daughter would walk Snow out into the alley to relieve himself then she and Snow would get in the car. This particular morning the man upstairs that had a medium size black dog, had his dog out too but unleashed. We didn't see her at first until the dog approached Snow and sized him up, Snow checked her out too. The next thing you know this dog starts fighting Snow. I jump out of the car and tell my Daughter not to put her hand by the dogs as I'm calling the Owner to get his dog off of my dog. He rushes over and apologizes, I voice your dog should be on a leash! This may sound crazy but the dogs from the suburbs don't fight each other when they approach one another, they sniff each other or sometimes if it is another dog of the same sex they may bark at each other. It may be because of the way pet Owners interact with their pets in the community, things like going to dog parks etc. Snow is used to this type of behavior, it through him and us off guard when this dog attacked him, especially with it being a female dog and not a male dog. No offense to my Detroit citizens but I thought to myself, stupid Detroit dog!

Another time I hear a knock at the door which surprised me because no one knew we were here and no one could enter the building without a remote. I knew if it was one of the people from Threat Management they would have called first. I ask who is it as I look through the peephole, it is a young Caucasian woman who says through the door, I live upstairs and my friend used to live here in your place and he died, she went on, can I come in just to stand in his old place. I open the door for her and she walked in and with tear rimmed eyes visually looked around as she stood there then asked could she step in this one room right off the door where he left his initials. I say ok as I walk in the room with her I can tell and smell that she was intoxicated. Then she thanked me and left. I told Commander Brown about the incident and he told me not to let anyone else in no matter what.

Commander Brown tells me that Threat Management is not renewing the lease for that safehouse so I won't be able to stay there after that month. I tell him I'm thankful for the time we were allowed to stay there. Now we have to move again. This time I go to a Motel 6 in a suburb about the same distance from the girl's school but in another direction and in a much safer environment. I stay there and pay a monthly rate. I take a job at Red Lobster to help with paying for the motel. We ended up staying there several months.

I finally spoke to my Mother who said it was not her idea nor did she want to do it. She said she gave me the letter because my Sister told her too. I couldn't stay mad at my Mom plus I knew she was sad and worried about that whole situation. Despite it all, I love her and didn't want her to worry so I started back talking to her. I was still mad at my Sister but later on that year, I ended up forgiving her and talking back to her too.

When the first year after my attack rolls around I find myself having panic and anxiety attacks. It actually started on June 9th I seem to keep dropping everything. I can't focus, I'm nervous and jittery. Fear creeps up and grips me on the 10th and I cannot control my emotions. I feel really sad...

HUMS does its first fundraiser cruise in September of 2008. It was great. I drove with a group of people who agreed to leave a few days early and stop in Tennessee to explore caverns then go on the cruise. Once the cruise ended, we met up with a dear friend of mine; Mr. Lonnie Ward Jr. in Florida then visited friends there before heading to Atlanta to stay over night. On our way home I was thinking I cannot keep returning to Michigan, I had a wonderful two weeks but now I'm just down about going back so I decide that we are going to move to Georgia with my oldest while we save up to get our own place. I pray and ask if it is the will of my Father in heaven and I ask if it is your will Lord then let me be allowed to transfer from this Red Lobster to one in the Atlanta area. I followed the necessary channels and everything worked out! I moved two weeks after I came off the cruise. Most of my things were in storage so I just had to pack me and the girl's things and Snow.

I could have probably saved my money from the restaurant and the money from the cost of the motel and rented a place back in

Michigan but in my heart I knew I could no longer stay there. It would end up being one and a half years of being homeless and staying with family or in a motel.

I started attending church at Dunamis Outreach Ministries' Atlanta location. They don't have the ministry training program out here so I didn't finish the program I had started in Detroit. However I knew this was the season for my move to Georgia. The Atlanta ministry is under the leadership of Pastors and Doctors Mark and Tamara Goodridge. The girls and I along with my three Grandsons go there. It is held in a small environment that is filled with love. The members there are very nice and my Pastors are intelligent, down to earth, caring people who also teach good doctrine. It is nice I like it here; it feels like a close knit family. The only thing missing is the awesome praise and worship part of the service that I'm used to at my Detroit Dunamis church home. They have sincere praise and worship but it is just different from what I am accustomed too.

CHAPTER 9

INTERNET NEWS ARTICLE

The following article was written to be published on an internet newspaper site that had featured an article about my story.

My niece had mentioned to me that my story was on several internet sites and to my surprise, she was right.....this is a copy of my response.

VIOLENCE NEEDS TO STOP AGAINST WOMEN

He kept trying to cut my throat, then he stabbed me in my eye....... sadly this is apart of my story. It was also the story featured here on June 14th, 2007. The headlines read "Michigan Man Arrested For Beating, Stabbing And Raping Woman". I actually cried when I heard that my story was all over the news, in the paper and even on the internet. What happened to me was so painful and personal and I felt that my life had been exposed to the whole world. Now I tell my story to help others. I'm a survivor of attempted murder and rape. Charles Blue Jr. decided he wanted to murder me than commit suicide. He and I dated in early 2006 then ended our dating that same year but remained friends. My ending our friendship on June 3rd of this year is the beginning of my nightmare.

The following Sunday night he lured me over to his apartment, then proceeded to punch me nonstop in the face with all his might. He was very angry and enraged and told me that he tricked me into coming over so that he could cut my throat than cut his throat. He said that the only way we were leaving there was in body bags. He sliced my flesh open on my hand and arms which were up in a protective mode trying to shield my face from the blows he inflicted and to block him from cutting my throat. He tried several times to cut my throat open, however the knife that sliced me open easily everywhere else would not slice my neck. I truly believe that was God's intervention. He also stabbed me in my left eye. I felt the blade go into my eyeball and out. I thought my eye was going to deflate or gush fluids. He also raped me that night.

This is a very condensed version of my horrendous experience. Go to www.h-u-m-s.org to read or hear my interview of my whole story which includes how I got away. Read each page to see what the effects are of my sharing my story from comments placed in our guestbook and forum by women it's helped across our nation. See what I'm doing to bring victory out of tragedy! You see, I did not want to be a victim but I chose to be a survivor! One who reaches out to others who have been victimized. One who'd educate our nation and motivate our communities to get involved. One who'd fight to get tougher laws in place for abusers and offenders. One who'd reach out to the world to financially assist us in securing housing, building several centers and temporary shelters for women and their children as well as providing training, workshops and a TV show all in our efforts to help. Although we've started our first office in Michigan and then in Atlanta Georgia, we still plan to expand our organization across the country.

Now I want to share with you some of these other headlines similar to my headline above mentioned.

WXYZ CHANNEL 7

"Rape, Murder Charges for Dad in Baby Death" He also beat the Mother as they were on the way to the hospital with the baby. 12/03/07

"Husband Charged with Murder in Wife's Fatal Fall" 12/27/07

"Former boyfriend charged with murder in death of Eli Lilly drug representative" "Franklin (the victim) had filed a Police

report about threatening phone calls she received from a man she dated briefly." 12/08/07

"Five dead, including 3 children, in murder-suicide" LAYTONSVILLE, Md. (AP) - Police in Maryland say a man shot and killed his ex-Wife and their three children in a park yesterday before killing himself. 11/23/07

"Detroit-area EMT kills Wife, wounds Son, then kills self" 11/26/07

"Police find missing JSU student's body, charge ex-boyfriend with......" 11/29/07

"Grant Pleads Guilty to Mutilation" Stephen Grant mutilates his Wife, Tara 12/07/07

CHANNEL 4

"Woman Stabbed By Live-In Boyfriend" 10/24/07

"Woman Hospitalized After Being Beaten, Stabbed In Church" 10/03/07

"Man Arraigned On Suspicion Of Stabbing Ex-Wife, Son"

"Waitress Stabbed To Death At Orlando Denny's"

"A 40-year-old Denny's waitress was fatally stabbed in the neck and chest in front of dozens of customers and children at the tourist-filled International Drive..."

CANTON PUBLIC SAFETY WEBSITE:

June 12, 2007, Canton MI - Charles Blue, Jr., 38, of Canton, was arraigned this morning on charges of Assault with Intent to Murder, two counts of Criminal Sexual Conduct, and 1 count of Felonious Assault, in the attack of his estranged girlfriend.

WDIV Channel 4 "Man Charged In Beating, Rape Case"

These last headlines refer to my story and this is a picture of the man who tried to kill me. The Judge later added an additional CSC (criminal sexual conduct) count. Bringing the total counts against this man to five counts. On the day of finally going to trial, and after many court dates, Charles Blue took the plea bargain and pled guilty just before the trial was to start that morning. He only received fifteen to twenty five years although several of these counts carried life sentences. The five counts were reduced to three counts. I feel the twenty five years should have been the minimum and forty plus years the maximum. Laws need to be tougher.

The thing is, people just like you, who read or hear stories such as mine or like the headlines I've placed in this article, will sympathize for the moment and then you'll go on with your life. What you don't realize is that there is a person who is still hurting, still suffering in many ways including post traumatic stress syndrome/disorder, still battling fear among a long list of other distressful challenges. The crime in itself is horrific enough, however it is the aftermath that is a struggle to overcome. This is true of the victim if they survived, but if the person didn't live, then there is a family who is going through these things as well. Parents, children and loved ones stricken with pain, grief, sadness, hurt and a need to understand why. The healing process for victims and/or their families can last for years even with counseling.

Let me tell you what it is like from a survivor's prospective. My life changed drastically, I had not returned to my residence afterward, I went to my relative's home after being released from the hospital. I was overwhelmed with fear and was afraid to go outside of my family's home. I keep thinking he was still going to try to kill me, even though he was arrested immediately and bail was set very high. I thought he'd escape and come after me and so out of fear, I panicked and on Father's Day I had my family and friends along with their Wives and children move my things from my home and business into storage.

I had many other panic attacks besides the moving of my things. I didn't feel safe in this world, I felt so vulnerable. I remember walking up to the courthouse and passing men and women and thinking to myself "are they going to hurt me, is he/she going to hit me or kill me!" I would have to talk to myself inwardly and say "no Rhonda, it's alright, they're just walking by, it's ok" I'd have flashbacks of him trying to kill me every time I was alone or whenever I closed my eyes. I couldn't sleep, I had to take sleeping pills or I'd take vicodins for the pain and because it made me drowsy. Neither really worked, it made me close my eyes, but my mind keep thinking and reliving things. I would be very jumpy and easily startled. It took weeks for me to drive again because too many things are happening when you drive and it was as if I was a big ball of unsettled nerves and too jittery to focus and not panic.

I also had uncontrollable crying spells. I didn't even know why I was crying and could not stop. I also had days where I would be extremely sad. I could not control my emotions and on top of all of this, I couldn't focus or remember things. Even simple things like spelling easy words or what terms were used in mortgages, which was the business I'd been doing for several years. These were just some of the challenges I faced. Needless to say, I thought I was going absolutely CRAZY!

I started professional counseling which helped a lot. My Counselor explained so many things to me, like the fact I was going through post traumatic stress disorder/syndrome which normally will occur after such a trauma. She said everything that I've been feeling is also normal and that I wasn't going crazy, just healing. She said the healing journey could take years and even then I could still have flashbacks periodically. I will honestly tell you that I could see why people who've been through similar circumstances sometimes feel so defeated that they contemplate suicide or drug/alcohol use to cope with their state of mind. I certainly do not condone these types of negative means of coping with these issues; however I want you the readers to grasp the severity of the after effects on victims of violent crimes.

Please understand that I have always had a heart to help people. I've gotten involved in so many ways to make a difference in this world. For example, I've been a volunteer in my old community as an Auxiliary Police Officer; I've also been a foster Mom and have adopted two of my five Daughters. My point to this is that as much as I care about people and as much as I've gotten involved in helping others, I would have never ever thought that anyone who knew me would want to kill me. So I know that you probably feel that same way, but look at those headlines again. Don't you think that maybe just maybe these women thought the same way too?

Think about it, I'm almost willing to bet that if you're a woman reading this that you have experienced some form of abuse whether it is on a small or large scale. In the form of verbal, mental, or physical abuse or even sexual assault/abuse. If not than more than likely you know of someone who was. I feel this last statement holds true for every male or female reader of this article. I don't mean to be so blunt, but the fact is what we keep seeing on the news and reading about is REAL and is happening at an alarming rate. The other point I'll make is that these perpetrators are getting so bold in the murder or attempted murder of a woman that they'll do it right in front of other people, like the man at Denny's or the man who

77

stabbed his girlfriend to death in front of a neighbor's house that she fled to for help.

We have got to come together as a Nation and make a difference. I challenge you to do something in this fight to stop violence toward women. I pray that what you've read will stir something up on the inside of you. You see it's great that you'll probably leave a comment in the forum section here and perhaps on our website in our forum or guestbook, but then what will you do?

Here are the challenges I place before you and these are suggestions of ways you can make a difference:

•   Get financially involved with an Organization dedicated to the cause. Give a one time donation or to be more effective in this fight give on a regular monthly bases. Visit our website at www.h-u-m-s.org and support us in our endeavors or select another organization that's fighting for this cause.

•   Donate clothing, food etc. to a local Domestic Violence shelter.

•   Find out how you can help to get the laws changed to be more tougher on abusers and offenders.

•   Spread the word to others to get involved. Send them this article and tell them to please visit our website.

I thank God that I have faith to know that it is God who saved me that night and that it is Him who keeps me even now and leads me on this mission to help stop the violence against women.

Written by Rhonda Knight the "Blessed Survivor", Founder of Uplifting Hearts, Minds & Souls (H.U.M.S.)

Yes I know his real name is mentioned here, but that's ok, I wanted to leave the article just as it was written. Plus it was also mentioned in one of the letters written in chapter five, which I'm sure you notice too. But regardless of his name, his actions are what is important in recounting this story.

CHAPTER 10

EFFECTS OF ABUSE/ASSAULT

Post-Traumatic Stress Disorder

PTSD is not a rare or unusual occurrence, in fact, many people experience PTSD as a result of a traumatic experience such as rape or sexual assault. Post-traumatic Stress Disorder (PTSD) is a normal human reaction to an extreme or abnormal situation. Each person has a different threshold for what is perceived as a traumatic event.

You may be experiencing PTSD if, following an event where you experienced or were confronted with actual or threatened injury or a threat to your physical integrity, you have:

> ➢ shown symptoms of intense horror, helplessness, or fear
> ➢ experienced distressing memories of the event (e.g., flashbacks, including nightmares)
> ➢ regularly avoided things or triggers that remind you of the event (e.g., people, places, things, etc.)
> ➢ shown significant impairment or distress due to the event
> ➢ shown at least two symptoms of increased arousal (e.g., sleep difficulties, difficulty concentrating, hyper vigilance, an exaggerated startle response, or irritability or outburst of anger/rage)
> ➢ experienced these things for at least a month

The National Center for PTSD has extensive information on PTSD, including information on Coping with PTSD and tips on What You Can Do.

Coping with PTSD and Recommended Lifestyle Changes for PTSD Patients Joe Ruzek, Ph.D.

Coping with PTSD

Because PTSD symptoms seldom disappear completely, it is usually a continuing challenge for survivors of trauma to cope with PTSD symptoms and the problems they cause. Survivors often learn through treatment how to cope more effectively.

Recovery from PTSD is an ongoing, daily, gradual process. It doesn't happen through sudden insight or "cure." Healing doesn't mean that a survivor will forget traumatic experiences or have no emotional pain when remembering them. Some level of continuing reaction to memories is normal and reflects a normal body and mind. Recovery may lead to fewer reactions and reactions that are less intense. It may also lead to a greater ability to manage trauma-related emotions and to greater confidence in one's ability to cope.

When a trauma survivor takes direct action to cope with problems, he or she often gains a sense of personal power and control. Active coping means recognizing and accepting the impact of traumatic experiences and then taking concrete action to improve things.

Positive coping actions

Actions that help to reduce anxiety and lessen other distressing reactions. Positive coping actions also improve the situation in a way that does not harm the survivor further and in a way that lasts into the future. Positive coping methods include:

Learning about trauma and PTSD

It is useful for trauma survivors to learn more about PTSD and how it affects them. By learning that PTSD is common and that their problems are shared by hundreds of thousands of others, survivors recognize that they are not alone, weak, or crazy. When a survivor seeks treatment and learns to recognize and understand what upsets him or her, he or she is in a better position to cope with the symptoms of PTSD.

Talking to another person for support

When survivors are able to talk about their problems with others, something helpful often results. Of course, survivors must choose their support people carefully and clearly ask for what they need. With support from others, survivors may feel less alone, feel supported or understood, or receive concrete help with a problem situation. Often, it is best to talk to professional Counselors about issues related to the traumatic experience itself; they are more likely than friends or family to understand trauma and its effects. It is also helpful to seek support from a support group. Being in a group with others who have PTSD may help reduce one's sense of isolation, rebuild trust in others, and provide an important opportunity to contribute to the recovery of other survivors of trauma.

Talking to your Doctor about trauma and PTSD

Part of taking care of yourself means mobilizing the helping resources around you. Your Doctor can take care of your physical health better if he or she knows about your PTSD, and Doctors can often refer you to more specialized and expert help.

Practicing relaxation methods

These can include muscular relaxation exercises, breathing exercises, meditation, swimming, stretching, yoga, prayer, listening to quiet music, spending time in nature, and so on. While relaxation techniques can be helpful, they can sometimes increase distress by focusing attention on disturbing physical sensations or by reducing contact with the external environment. Be aware that while uncomfortable physical sensations may become more apparent when you are relaxed, in the long run, continuing with relaxation in a way that is tolerable (i.e., interspersed with music, walking, or other activities) helps reduce negative reactions to thoughts, feelings, and perceptions.

Increasing positive distracting activities

Positive recreational or work activities help distract a person from his or her memories and reactions. Artistic endeavors have also been a way for many trauma survivors to express their feelings in a positive, creative way. This can improve your mood, limit the harm caused by PTSD, and help you rebuild your life. It is important to emphasize that distraction alone is unlikely to facilitate recovery; active, direct coping with traumatic events and their impact is also important.

Calling a Counselor for help

Sometimes PTSD symptoms worsen and ordinary efforts at coping don't seem to work. Survivors may feel fearful or depressed. At these times, it is important to reach out and telephone a Counselor, who can help turn things around.

Taking prescribed medications to tackle PTSD

One tool that many with PTSD have found helpful is medication treatment. By taking medications, some survivors of trauma are able to improve their sleep, anxiety, irritability, anger, and urges to drink or use drugs.

Negative coping actions

Sadly some people go these ways but as you will read, it only hurts you more and makes matters worse...

Negative actions help to perpetuate problems. They may reduce distress immediately but short-circuit more permanent change. Some actions that may be immediately effective may also cause later problems, like smoking or drug use. These habits can become difficult to change. Negative coping methods can include isolation, use of drugs or alcohol, workaholism, violent behavior, angry intimidation of others, unhealthy eating, and different types of self-destructive behavior (e.g., attempting suicide). Before learning more effective and healthy coping methods, most people with PTSD try to cope with their distress and other reactions in ways that lead to more problems. The following are negative coping actions:

Use of alcohol or drugs

This may help wash away memories, increase social confidence, or induce sleep, but it causes more problems than it cures. Using alcohol or drugs can create a dependence on alcohol, harm one's judgment, harm one's mental abilities, cause problems in relationships with family and friends, and sometimes place a person at risk for suicide, violence, or accidents.

Social isolation

By reducing contact with the outside world, a trauma survivor may avoid many situations that cause him or her to feel afraid, irritable, or angry. However, isolation will also cause major problems. It will result in the loss of social support, friendships, and intimacy. It may breed further depression and fear. Less participation in positive activities leads to fewer opportunities for positive emotions and achievements.

Anger

Like isolation, anger can get rid of many upsetting situations by keeping people away. However, it also keeps away positive connections and help, and it can gradually drive away the important people in a person's life. It may lead to job problems, marital or relationship problems, and the loss of friendships.

Continuous avoidance

If you avoid thinking about the trauma or if you avoid seeking help, you may keep distress at bay, but this behavior also prevents you from making progress in how you cope with trauma and its consequences.

Recommended Lifestyle Changes – Taking Control

Those with PTSD need to take active steps to deal with their PTSD symptoms. Often, these steps involve making a series of thoughtful changes in one's lifestyle to reduce symptoms and improve quality of life. Positive lifestyle changes include:

Calling about treatment and joining a PTSD support group

It may be difficult to take the first step and join a PTSD treatment group. Survivors say to themselves, "What will happen there?

Nobody can help me anyway." In addition, people with PTSD find it hard to meet new people and trust them enough to open up. However, it can also be a great relief to feel that you have taken positive action. You may also be able to eventually develop a friendship with another survivor.

Increasing contact with other survivors of trauma

Other survivors of trauma are probably the best source of understanding and support. By joining a survivors organization or by otherwise increasing contact with other survivors, it is possible to reverse the process of isolation and distrust of others.

Reinvesting in personal relationships with family and friends

Most survivors of trauma have some kind of a relationship with a Son or Daughter, a Wife or Partner, or an old friend or work acquaintance. If you make the effort to reestablish or increase contact with that person, it can help you reconnect with others.

Changing neighborhoods

Survivors with PTSD usually feel that the world is a very dangerous place and that it is likely that they will be harmed again. It is not a good idea for people with PTSD to live in a high-crime area because it only makes those feelings worse and confirms their beliefs. If it is possible to move to a safer neighborhood, it is likely that fewer things will set off traumatic memories. This will allow the person to reconsider his or her personal beliefs about danger.

Refraining from alcohol and drug abuse

Many trauma survivors turn to alcohol and drugs to help them cope with PTSD. Although these substances may distract a person from his or her painful feelings and, therefore, may appear to help deal with symptoms, relying on alcohol and drugs always makes things worse in the end. These substances often hinder PTSD treatment and recovery. Rather than trying to beat an addiction by yourself, it is often easier to deal with addictions by joining a treatment program where you can be around others who are working on similar issues.

Starting an exercise program

It is important to see a Doctor before starting to exercise. However, if the Physician gives the OK, exercise in moderation can benefit those with PTSD. Walking, jogging, swimming, weight lifting, and other forms of exercise may reduce physical tension. They may distract the person from painful memories or worries and give him or her a break from difficult emotions. Perhaps most important, exercise can improve self-esteem and create feelings of personal control.

Starting to volunteer in the community

It is important to feel as though you are contributing to your community. When you are not working, you may not feel you have anything to offer others. One way survivors can reconnect with their communities is to volunteer. You can help with youth programs, medical services, literacy programs, community sporting activities, etc.

Complex PTSD

Diagnosis necessary to describe the symptoms experienced by survivors of long-term trauma such as child sexual abuse and prostitution.

Dr. Judith Herman developed the concept of Complex PTSD. She argues that this new diagnosis is necessary to describe the symptoms experienced by survivors of long-term trauma such as child sexual abuse, prostitution, and organized child exploitation rings.

The National Center for Post-Traumatic Stress Disorder has a very helpful Fact Sheet on Complex PTSD.

Julia M. Whealin, Ph.D. and Laurie Slone, Ph.D.

Differences between the effects of short-term trauma and the effects of chronic trauma...

The diagnosis of PTSD accurately describes the symptoms that result when a person experiences a short-lived trauma. For example, car accidents, natural disasters, and rape are considered traumatic events of time-limited duration. However, chronic traumas continue or repeat for months or years at a time. Clinicians and researchers have found that the current PTSD diagnosis often does not capture the severe psychological harm that occurs with such prolonged, repeated trauma. For example, ordinary, healthy people who experience chronic trauma can experience changes in their self-concept and the way they adapt to stressful events. Dr. Judith Herman of Harvard University suggests that a new diagnosis, called Complex PTSD, is needed to describe the symptoms of long-term trauma. Another name sometimes used to describe this cluster of symptoms is: Disorders of Extreme Stress Not Otherwise Specified (DESNOS).

Because results from the DSM-IV Field Trials indicated that 92% of individuals with Complex PTSD/DESNOS also met criteria for PTSD, Complex PTSD was not added as a separate diagnosis. Complex PTSD may indicate a need for special treatment considerations.

What are examples of types of captivity that are associated with chronic trauma?

Judith Herman notes that during long-term traumas, the victim is generally held in a state of captivity, physically or emotionally. In these situations the victim is under the control of the perpetrator and unable to flee.

Examples of captivity include:

- Concentration camps

- Prisoner of War camps

- Prostitution brothels

- Long-term domestic violence

- Long-term, severe physical abuse

- Child sexual abuse

- Organized child exploitation rings

What are the symptoms of Complex PTSD?

The first requirement for the diagnosis is that the individual experienced a prolonged period (months to years) of total control by another. The other criteria are symptoms that tend to result from chronic victimization. Those symptoms include:

Alterations in emotional regulation

This may include symptoms such as persistent sadness, suicidal thoughts, explosive anger, or inhibited anger

Alterations in consciousness

This includes things such as forgetting traumatic events, reliving traumatic events, or having episodes in which one feels detached from one's mental processes or body

Changes in self-perception

This may include a sense of helplessness, shame, guilt, stigma, and a sense of being completely different than other human beings

Alterations in the perception of the perpetrator

For example; attributing total power to the perpetrator or becoming preoccupied with the relationship to the perpetrator, including a preoccupation with revenge

Alterations in relations with others

Variations in personal relations including isolation, distrust, or a repeated search for a rescuer.

Changes in one's system of meanings

This may include a loss of sustaining faith or a sense of hopelessness and despair

What other difficulties do those with Complex PTSD tend to experience?

- Survivors may avoid thinking and talking about trauma-related topics because the feelings associated with the trauma are often overwhelming.

- Survivors may use alcohol and substance abuse as a way to avoid and numb feelings and thoughts related to the trauma

- Survivors may also engage in self-mutilation and other forms of self-harm.

There is a tendency to blame the victim.

A person who has been abused repeatedly is sometimes mistaken as someone who has a "weak character."

Because of their chronic victimization, in the past, survivors have been misdiagnosed by mental-health providers as having Borderline, Dependent, or Masochistic Personality Disorder. When survivors are faulted for the symptoms they experience as a result of victimization, they are being unjustly blamed.

Researchers hope that a new diagnosis will prevent Clinicians, the public, and those who suffer from trauma from mistakenly blaming survivors for their symptoms.

Summary

The current PTSD diagnosis often does not capture the severe psychological harm that occurs with prolonged, repeated trauma. For example, long-term trauma may impact a healthy person's self-concept and adaptation. The symptoms of such prolonged trauma have been mistaken for character weakness. Research is currently underway to determine if the Complex PTSD diagnosis is the best way to categorize the symptoms of patients who have suffered prolonged trauma.

Recommended Reading

Trauma and Recovery: The Aftermath of Violence from Domestic Abuse to Political Terror, by Judith Herman, M.D. (1997). Basic Books; ISBN 0465087302

References

Ford, J. D. (1999). Disorders of extreme stress following war-zone military trauma: Associated features of Posttraumatic Stress Disorder or comorbid but distinct syndromes? Journal of Consulting and Clinical Psychology, 67, 3-12.

Herman, J. (1997). Trauma and recovery: The aftermath of violence from domestic abuse to political terror. New York: Basic Books.

Roth, S., Newman, E., Pelcovitz, D., van der Kolk, B., & Mandel, F. S. (1997). Complex PTSD in victims exposed to sexual and physical abuse: Results from the DSM-IV field trial for Posttraumatic Stress Disorder. Journal of Traumatic Stress, 10, 539-555.

Battered Woman Syndrome

A controversial concept, battered woman syndrome is a model that was developed by Dr. Lenore E. Walker to describe the mindset and emotional state of a battered woman. NOTE: While men are also victims of domestic violence, the concept of battered woman syndrome typically refers only to women. For this reason, the following description will follow this format but recognizes that the same or a similar mindset could hold true for battered men as well.

A battered woman is a woman who has experienced at least two complete battering cycles as described in dating and domestic violence.

Battered women stay in these dangerous relationships for a variety of reasons including:

> still being positively reinforced by the "honeymoon" phase of the battering cycle
> economic dependence upon the batterer
> belief that they can keep the peace
> fear of danger if she were to leave
> threats made by the batterer to hurt her or her children if she left
> loss of self-esteem
> depression or loss of psychological energy necessary to leave

According to Walker's *The Battered Woman Syndrome* (p. 95-97, 1984), there are four general characteristics of the syndrome:

1. The woman believes that the violence was or is her fault.

2. The woman has an inability to place responsibility for the violence elsewhere.

3. The woman fears for her life and/or her children's lives.

4. The woman has an irrational belief that the abuser is omnipresent and omniscient.

More recently, Battered Woman Syndrome has also been associated with <u>post-traumatic stress disorder</u> in that domestic violence involves exposure to severe trauma and so the reactions of a battered woman may be due to flashbacks or other intrusive experiences from previous traumatic events so that the woman believes that she is in danger, even if she is not.

This syndrome has been used as an explanation for reactions to abusive situations in court cases but has also been used as an educational tool in order to raise the awareness of the impact that domestic violence can have on women.

Body Memories

What are Somatic (Body) Memories?

Body memories are when the stress of the memories of the abuse experienced by an individual take the form of physical problems that cannot be explained by the usual means (medical examinations, etc.).

These maladies are often called "psychosomatic symptoms" which does not, as many people think, mean that it is "in your head." Rather, it means that the symptoms are due to the connection between the mind and the body.

Physical problems that can come of these somatic memories include headaches, migraines, stomach difficulties, light headedness/dizziness, hot/cold flashes, grinding of teeth, sleep disorders, etc.

These maladies can often be frustrating for the survivor of a sexual assault who is experiencing them as they are difficult to diagnose and cure and may add to the difficult experience of recovery.

Borderline Personality Disorder

Borderline Personality Disorder is one of the most controversial mental illness diagnoses in Psychology today. There are several different theories as to why an individual develops Borderline Personality Disorder and how it should be treated (or even if it can be treated).

What is Borderline Personality Disorder?

While people with Borderline Personality Disorder are often funny, witty, intelligent, and the life of the party, they are also known for their inconsistent behavior and often chaotic lifestyle.

There are a number of different definitions of Borderline Personality Disorder but most agree it can include:

> ➢ a fear of being abandoned or alone which can lead to frantic efforts to avoid such a state of being
> ➢ intense and unstable relationships which swing between idealization and devaluation
> ➢ unstable self-image or sense of self

- impulsivity (e.g., substance abuse, reckless sexual encounters, binge eating, reckless driving, extreme spending)
- suicidal or self-mutilating thoughts or behaviors
- extremely unstable moods that last from a few hours to a few days
- inappropriate or overwhelming anger and rage
- transient, stress-related paranoia or dissociative symptoms
- hypersensitivity to any nonverbal communication and expression

For more information, visit the National Institute of Mental Health's article on Borderline Personality Disorder.

References:

Diagnostic and Statistical Manual of Mental Disorders, Fourth Edition, Text Revision (p.710, 2000).

National Institute of Mental Health. Borderline Personality Disorder: Raising questions, finding answers. Bethesda (MD).

Depression

There are many emotional and psychological reactions that victims of domestic/dating violence, rape and sexual assault can experience. One of the most common of these is depression.

The term "depression" can be confusing since many of the symptoms are experienced by people as normal reactions to events in their life. At some point or another during one's life, everyone feels sad or "blue." This also means that recognizing depression can be difficult since the symptoms can easily be attributed to other causes. These feelings are perfectly normal, especially during difficult times.

Depression becomes something more than just normal feelings of sadness when the symptoms last for more than two weeks. Therefore, if you experience five or more of the symptoms of depression over the course of two weeks you should consider talking to your Doctor about what you are experiencing.

The symptoms for depression include:

- ➤ Prolonged sadness or unexplained crying spells
- ➤ Change in appetite with significant weight loss (without dieting) or weight gain
- ➤ Loss of energy or persistent fatigue or lethargy
- ➤ Significant change in sleep patterns (insomnia, sleeping too much, fitful sleep, etc.)
- ➤ Loss of interest and pleasure in activities previously enjoyed, social withdrawal.
- ➤ Feelings of worthlessness, hopelessness, or inappropriate guilt
- ➤ Pessimism or indifference
- ➤ Unexplained aches and pains (headaches, stomachaches)
- ➤ Inability to concentrate, indecisiveness
- ➤ Irritability, worry, anger, agitation, or anxiety
- ➤ Recurring thoughts of death or suicide

Depression can affect anyone of any age, gender, race, ethnicity, or religion. Depression is not a sign of weakness, and it is not something that someone can make him/herself "snap out of."

_____

Reference:

American Psychiatric Association, Diagnostic and Statistical Manual of Mental Disorders: Text Revision, fourth edition, 2000

Suicide

If you are currently thinking about suicide, or know someone who is, please reach out for help.

If someone you know is thinking about suicide

Get help!

- ➤ Talk to someone you trust
- ➤ Do you have a friend or relative that you can talk to?
- ➤ Do you have a Counselor or Therapist that you can call?
- ➤ Is there someone else in your life that you can talk to (a religious Leader, Coach or Teacher)?
- ➤ Suicide hotline
- ➤ If there's no one in your life that you feel comfortable talking to about your suicidal thoughts, call the National Suicide Prevention Lifeline at (800) 273-TALK.
- ➤ Your call will be confidential, and the Counselors there can help!
- ➤ Call 911 or go to the hospital
- ➤ If you have already taken steps to harm yourself or feel that you can't stop yourself from committing suicide, call 911 or go to the emergency room.
- ➤ Tell the person on the phone or the front desk at the emergency room that you are suicidal.
- ➤ If you are not thinking about committing suicide right now, but have thought about it in the past or are afraid that you might start, please get help!
- ➤ Reach out to friends, family or someone you trust. Let them know that you are going through a rough time.
- ➤ If you aren't ready to talk to someone face-to-face, call the National Suicide Prevention Lifeline any time at (800) 273-TALK.

The Counselors there can talk to you about ways to resolve the situation that has made you think about suicide and can connect you with resources to help you.

- ➤ Survivors of sexual assault can also call (800) 656-HOPE
- ➤ Survivors of dating/domestic violence can also call (800) 799-SAFE
- ➤ Find a Counselor or Therapist who can help you figure out how to resolve your situation.
- ➤ If you have health insurance, your insurance company can give you the number of a Counselor.
- ➤ If you are a Student, the school Counselor or counseling center will have Counselors that you can talk to.
- ➤ If you work, or if your spouse works, you may have access to an employee assistance program that provides counseling. Ask your human resources person.

- ➢ If you don't have health insurance, or none of these options works, call your local health department (you can find their phone number in the Blue Pages of your phone book). They can connect you with Counselors.
- ➢ Get rid of the means. If you have been thinking about committing suicide and you have obtained the means to commit suicide, please get rid of it. If you have a gun, give it to someone you trust. If you have pills, flush them down the toilet. Do whatever it takes to keep you safe!

Remember: if you have taken steps to harm yourself or you feel that you cannot avoid hurting yourself, call 911 or go to the emergency room!

Dissociative Identity Disorder

Before explaining what Dissociative Identity Disorder (formerly known as Multiple Personality Disorder) is, we first must define dissociation.

Dissociation is a mental process in which a person's thoughts and feelings may be separated from his or her immediate reality.

Most mental health practitioners believe that dissociation exists on a continuum. At one end of the continuum, are instances of dissociation that many people experience such as daydreaming or highway hypnosis. At the other end, though, is chronic and complex dissociation which may impair an individual's ability to function in the "real" world.

According to the Diagnostic and Statistical Manual of Mental Disorders, Fourth Edition, Text Revision (p. 529, 2000), Dissociative Identity Disorder (DID) is:

A. The presence of two or more distinct identities or personality states (each with its own relatively enduring pattern of perceiving, relating to, and thinking about the environment and self).

B. At least two of these identities or personality states recurrently take control of the person's behavior.

C. Inability to recall important personal information that is too extensive to be explained by ordinary forgetfulness.

D. The disturbance is not due to the direct physiological effects of a substance (e.g., blackouts or chaotic behavior during Alcohol Intoxication) or a general medical condition (e.g., complex partial seizures). NOTE: In children, the symptoms are not attributable to imaginary playmates or other fantasy play.

While the causes of DID are not entirely known, it is believed that the disorder stems from physical or sexual abuse in childhood. It is believed that children develop this disorder when during abusive situations they slip into dissociative states in order to remove themselves from the situation. If the abuse continues over time, it is believed that children may then begin to split into alter identities during these times of dissociation.

For more information, visit the National Alliance on Mental Illness's article on Dissociative Identity Disorder.

Reference:

Diagnostic and Statistical Manual of Mental Disorders, Fourth Edition, Text Revision

Flashbacks

Flashbacks are when memories of past traumas feel as if they are taking place in the current moment.

These memories can take many forms: dreams, sounds, smells, images, body sensations, or overwhelming emotions. This re-experience of the trauma often seems to come from nowhere and, therefore, blurs the lines between past and present, leaving the individual feeling anxious, scared, powerless, or any other emotions that they felt at the time of the trauma.

Some flashbacks are mild and brief, a passing moment, while others may be powerful and last a long time. Many times the individual does not even realize that he or she is having a flashback and may feel faint or dissociate.

What Helps During a Flashback?

If you realize that you are in the middle of a flashback:

> Tell yourself that you are having a flashback and remind yourself that the actual event is over and you survived.
> Breathe. Take slow, deep breaths by putting your hand on your stomach and taking deep enough breaths that your hand moves out with the inhalations and in with the exhalations. This is important because when we panic our body begins to take short, shallow breaths and the decrease in oxygen that accompanies this change increases our panicked state. So increasing the oxygen in our system can help us to get out of the anxious state we are in.
> Return to the present. Take time to use your five senses to establish where you are in the present. Look around you and take note of the colors in the room. Listen to the sounds that are happening around you. Smell the smells that are in the room with you. Feel the clothes on your skin and take note of how different parts of your body feel (hands, feet, etc.).
> Recognize what would make you feel more safe. Wrap yourself in a blanket, shut yourself in a room, whatever it takes to feel as if you are secure.
> Get the support of people you can trust. If you can, ask someone for help and support in this time of vulnerability.
> Take the time to recover. Let yourself have the time to get back to feeling comfortable and in the present. This may take a while and that is ok. If you like, take a nap, some time for yourself, or whatever it is that would help you feel safe and more comfortable.
> Be good to yourself. Know that you are not crazy and are not doing anything wrong- it takes time to heal.

Rape Trauma Syndrome

Rape Trauma Syndrome is a common reaction to a rape or sexual assault. It is the human reaction to an unnatural or extreme event.

There are three phases to Rape Trauma Syndrome

1. Acute Phase

This phase occurs immediately after the assault and usually lasts a few days to several weeks. In this phase individuals can have many reactions but they typically fall into three categories of reactions:

1. Expressed- This is when the survivor is openly emotional. He or she may appear agitated or hysterical; he or she may suffer from crying spells or anxiety attacks.

2. Controlled- This is when the survivor appears to be without emotion and acts as if "nothing happened" and "everything is fine." This appearance of calm may be shock.

3. Shocked Disbelief- This is when the survivor reacts with a strong sense of disorientation. He or she may have difficulty concentrating, making decisions, or doing everyday tasks. He or she may also have poor recall of the assault.

2. The Outward Adjustment Phase

During this phase the individual resumes what appears to be his or her "normal" life but inside is suffering from considerable turmoil. In this phase there are five primary coping techniques:

1. Minimization- Pretends that "everything is fine" or that "it could have been worse."

2. Dramatization- Cannot stop talking about the assault and it is what dominates their life and identity.

3. Suppression- Refuses to discuss acts as if it did not happen.

4. Explanation- Analyzes what happened- what the individual did, what the rapist was thinking/feeling.

5. Flight- Tries to escape the pain (moving, changing jobs, changing appearance, changing relationships, etc.).

There are many symptoms or behaviors that appear during this phase including:

> Continuing anxiety
> Severe mood swings
> Sense of helplessness
> Persistent fear or phobia
> Depression
> Rage
> Difficulty sleeping (nightmares, insomnia, etc.)
> Eating difficulties (nausea, vomiting, compulsive eating, etc.)
> Denial
> Withdrawal from friends, family, activities
> Hyper vigilance
> Reluctance to leave house and/or go places that remind the individual of the assault
> Sexual problems
> Difficulty concentrating
> Flashbacks

All of these symptoms and behaviors may make the individual more willing to seek counseling and/or to discuss the assault.

3.   The Resolution Phase

During this phase the assault is no longer the central focus of the individual's life. While he or she may recognize that he or she will never forget the assault; the pain and negative outcomes lessen over time. Often the individual will begin to accept the rape as part of his or her life and chooses to move on.

NOTE: This model assumes that individuals will take steps forward and backwards in their healing process and that while there are phases it is not a linear progression and will be different for every person.

Effects of Sexual Assault continued...

Sexual assault is an incredibly personal and destructive crime. Its effects on victims and their loved ones can be felt psychologically, emotionally, and physically. They can be brief in duration or last a very long time. It is important to remember that there is no one "normal" reaction to sexual assault. Every individual's response will be different depending on the situation. In this section, we have explained some of the more common effects that a victim may experience.

Adult Survivors of Childhood Sexual Assault

There are many reactions that survivors of rape and sexual assault can have. But for adult survivors of childhood abuse there are reactions that may either be different or stronger than for other survivors. CAVEAT: The following descriptions are meant to serve as a general guideline for how a victim of sexual assault might react in a time of pain or crisis. It is important to recognize, however, that each victim of sexual assault will have his or her own life experiences and personality that will influence how he or she react to the assault.

Reactions

There are many reactions that survivors of rape and sexual assault can have. But for adult survivors of childhood abuse there are reactions that may either be different or stronger than for other survivors. These include:

Setting Limits/Boundaries

Because your personal boundaries were invaded when you were young by someone you trusted and depended on, you may have trouble understanding that you have the right to control what happens to you.

Memories/Flashbacks

Like many survivors, you may experience flashbacks.

Anger

This is often the most difficult emotion for an adult survivor of childhood sexual abuse to get in touch with.

As a child your anger was powerless and had little to no effect on the actions of your abuser. For this reason you may not feel confident that you anger will be useful or helpful.

Grieving/Mourning

Being abused as a child means the loss of many things- childhood experiences, trust, innocence, normal relationship with family members (especially if the abuser was a family member).

You must be allowed to name those losses, grieve them, and then bury them.

Guilt, Shame, and Blame

You may carry a lot of guilt because you may have experienced pleasure or because you did not try to stop the abuse.

There may have been silence surrounding the abuse that led to feelings of shame.

It is important for you to understand that it was the adult who abused his/her position of Authority and should be held accountable, not you.

Trust

Learning to trust again may be very difficult for you.

You may find that you go from one extreme to the other, not trusting at all to trusting too much.

Coping Skills

You have undoubtedly developed skills in order to cope with the trauma.

Some of these are healthy (possibly separating yourself from family members, seeking out counseling, etc.)

Some are not (drinking or drug abuse, promiscuous sexual activity, etc.)

Self-esteem/Isolation

Low self-esteem is a result of all of the negative messages you received and internalized from your abusers.

Because entering into an intimate relationship involves trust, respect, love, and the ability to share, you may flee from intimacy or hold on too tightly for fear of losing the relationship.

Sexuality

You likely have to deal with the fact that your first initiation into sex came as a result of sexual abuse.

You may experience the return of body memories while engaging in a sexual activity with another person. Such memories may interfere in your ability to engage in sexual relationships which may leave you feeling frightened, frustrated, or ashamed.

Reference

This section was adapted from materials provided by the Texas Association Against Sexual Assault.

More Effects of Rape

Victims of sexual assault are:

> ➢ 3 times more likely to suffer from depression.
> ➢ 6 times more likely to suffer from post-traumatic stress disorder.
> ➢ 13 times more likely to abuse alcohol.
> ➢ 26 times more likely to abuse drugs.
> ➢ 4 times more likely to contemplate suicide.

Pregnancy

If you were recently raped, you may have concerns about becoming pregnant from the attack. If the assault happened a long time ago, you may have concerns about a pregnancy that resulted from the assault.

If you were recently assaulted:

The decision of what to do is yours to make. If you need additional information in order to make a decision, consider:

➢ Talking to a trusted friend or family member
➢ Talking to a support group
➢ Talking to a specialized Counselor/Therapist
➢ Talking to your Pastor

If you were assaulted in the past:

If you were assaulted in the past and there was a resulting pregnancy, you may have some residual feelings about the pregnancy. It is important to understand that any of these (and other) feelings are normal.

Pregnancies Resulting from Rape

In 2004-2005, 64,080 women were raped. According to medical reports; the incidence of pregnancy for one-time unprotected sexual intercourse is 5%. By applying the pregnancy rate to 64,080 women, RAINN estimates that there were 3,204 pregnancies as a result of rape during that period.

This calculation does not account for the following factors which could lower the actual number of pregnancies:

➢ Rape, as defined by the NCVS, is forced sexual intercourse. Forced sexual intercourse means vaginal, oral, or anal penetration by offender(s). This category includes incidents where the penetration is from a foreign object such as a bottle. Certain types of rape under this definition cannot cause pregnancy.

- ➤ Some victims of rape may be utilizing birth control methods, such as the pill, which will prevent pregnancy.
- ➤ Some rapists may wear condoms in an effort to avoid DNA detection.
- ➤ Victims of rape may not be able to become pregnant for medical or age-related reasons.

This calculation does not account for the following factors which could raise the actual number of pregnancies:

- ➤ Medical estimates of a 5% pregnancy rate are for one-time, unprotected sexual intercourse. Some victimizations may include multiple incidents of intercourse.
- ➤ Because of methodology, NCVS does not measure the victimization of Americans age 12 or younger. Rapes of these young people could results in pregnancies not accounted for in RAINN's estimates.

References

1.   National Institute of Justice & Centers for Disease Control & Prevention. Prevalence, Incidence and Consequences of Violence Against Women Survey. 1998.

2.   U.S. Department of Justice. 2003 National Crime Victimization Survey. 2003.

3.   U.S. Department of Justice. 2004 National Crime Victimization Survey. 2004.

4.   1998 Commonwealth Fund Survey of the Health of Adolescent Girls. 1998.

5.   U.S. Department of Health & Human Services, Administration for Children and Families. 1995 Child Maltreatment Survey. 1995.

6.   U.S. Bureau of Justice Statistics. 2000 Sexual Assault of Young Children as Reported to Law Enforcement. 2000.

7. World Health Organization. 2002.

8. U.S. Department of Justice. 2005 National Crime Victimization Survey. 2005.

MOST OF THE INFORMATION IN THIS CHAPTER WAS OBTAINED FROM THE RAINN (Rape, Abuse & Incest National Network) WEBSITE

OCD

What is OCD

Obsessive-compulsive disorder (OCD) is an anxiety disorder characterized by uncontrollable, unwanted thoughts and repetitive, ritualized behaviors you feel compelled to perform. If you have OCD, you probably recognize that your obsessive thoughts and compulsive behaviors are irrational – but even so, you feel unable to resist them and break free.

Like a needle getting stuck on an old record, obsessive-compulsive disorder (OCD) causes the brain to get stuck on a particular thought or urge. For example, you may check the stove twenty times to make sure it's really turned off, you're your hands until they're scrubbed raw, or drive around for hours to make sure that the bump you heard while driving wasn't a person you ran over.

Understanding obsessions and compulsions

Obsessions are involuntary, seemingly uncontrollable thoughts, images, or impulses that occur over and over again in your mind. You don't want to have these ideas – in fact, you know that they don't make any sense. But you can't stop them. Unfortunately, these obsessive thoughts are usually disturbing and distracting.

Compulsions are behaviors or rituals that you feel driven to act out again and again. Usually, compulsions are performed in an attempt to make obsessions go away. For example, if you're afraid of contamination, you might develop elaborate cleaning rituals. However, the relief never lasts. In fact, the obsessive thoughts usually come back stronger. And the compulsive behaviors often end up causing anxiety themselves as they become more demanding and time-consuming.

Most people with obsessive-compulsive disorder fall into one of the following categories:

> ➤ Washers are afraid of contamination. They usually have cleaning or hand-washing compulsions.
> ➤ Checkers repeatedly check things (oven turned off, door locked, etc.) that they associate with harm or danger.
> ➤ Doubters and sinners are afraid that if everything isn't perfect or done just right something terrible will happen or they will be punished.
> ➤ Counters and arrangers are obsessed with order and symmetry. They may have superstitions about certain numbers, colors, or arrangements.
> ➤ Hoarders fear that something bad will happen if they throw anything away. They compulsively hoard things that they don't need or use.

Just because you have obsessive thoughts or perform compulsive behaviors does **NOT** mean that you have obsessive-compulsive disorder. Many people have mild obsessions or compulsions that are strange or irrational, but they're still able to lead their lives without much disruption. But with obsessive-compulsive disorder, these thoughts and behaviors cause tremendous distress, take up a lot of time, and interfere with your daily routine, job, or relationships.

Signs and symptoms of obsessive-compulsive disorder (OCD)

Most people with obsessive-compulsive disorder (OCD) have both obsessions and compulsions, but some people experience just one or the other. The symptoms of OCD may wax and wane over time. Often, the symptoms get worse in times of stress.

Common obsessive thoughts in OCD include:

> ➤ Fear of being contaminated by germs or dirt or contaminating others

- ➢ Fear of causing harm to yourself or others
- ➢ Intrusive sexually explicit or violent thoughts and images
- ➢ Excessive focus on religious or moral ideas
- ➢ Fear of losing or not having things you might need
- ➢ Order and symmetry: the idea that everything must line up "just right."
- ➢ Superstitions; excessive attention to something considered lucky or unlucky
- ➢ Common compulsive behaviors in OCD include:
- ➢ Excessive double-checking of things, such as locks, appliances, and switches.
- ➢ Repeatedly checking in on loved ones to make sure they're safe.
- ➢ Counting, tapping, repeating certain words, or doing other senseless things to reduce anxiety.
- ➢ Spending a lot of time washing or cleaning.
- ➢ Ordering, evening out, or arranging things "just so."
- ➢ Praying excessively or engaging in rituals triggered by religious fear.
- ➢ Accumulating "junk" such as old newspapers, magazines, and empty food containers, or other things you don't have a use for.

OCD may be combined with or complicated by other symptoms - such as symptoms associated with **trauma**, schizophrenia, depression, **sexual abuse** and bipolar disorder. If OCD affects you - or someone close to you - get help - before your condition worsens.

Sometimes victims of trauma will demonstrate some OCD behaviors. Example; I have to have things in order around me; I constantly straighten out the pillows on my sofas or make sure the lamp shades are straight etc. My jokester of a Daughter, Mignon will come over and rearrange the items on my fireplace mantle and then after she's long gone, when I notice it I rush over and put things back in order. I have to have order; it gives me a sense of being able to control something in my life. I also check things, like is the door locked, did I remember to cut off the stove etc. the locked doors is because of a need to feel safe and the stove incidents has to do with my fear of my memory issues.

Dissociative Disorders

What are dissociative disorders?

A dissociative disorder is the breakdown of one's perception of his/her surroundings, memory, identity, or consciousness.

There are four main kinds of dissociative disorders:

1. Dissociative amnesia

2. Dissociative fugue

3. Dissociative identity disorder (previously called multiple personality disorder)

4. Depersonalization disorder

What are the main characteristics of each dissociative disorder?

Dissociative amnesia:

A dissociative amnesia may be present when a person is unable to remember important personal information, which is usually associated with a traumatic event in his/her life. The loss of memory creates gaps in this individual's personal history. Memory loss that's more extensive than normal forgetfulness and can't be explained by a physical or neurological condition is the main symptom of this condition. Sudden-onset amnesia following a traumatic event, such as a car accident is rare. More commonly, conscious recall of traumatic periods, events or people in your life especially from childhood is simply absent from your memory.

Dissociative fugue:

A dissociative fugue may be present when a person impulsively wanders or travels away from home and upon arrival in the new location is unable to remember his/her past. The individual's personal identity is lost because that person is confused about who he/she is. The travel from home generally occurs following a stressful event. The person in the fugue appears to be functioning normally to other people. However, after the fugue experience, the individual may not be able to recall what happened during the fugue state. The condition is usually diagnosed when relatives find their lost family member living in another community with a new identity.

Dissociative identity disorder:

Discussed earlier in the chapter.

Depersonalization disorder:

Feelings of detachment or estrangement from one's self are signs of depersonalization. Although these feelings are difficult to describe, individuals with this disorder will report feeling as if they are living in a dream or watching themselves on a movie screen. They feel separated from themselves or outside their own bodies. Time may seem to slow down, and the world may seem unreal. Symptoms may last only a few moments or may come and go over many years. People with this disorder feel like they are "going crazy" and they frequently become anxious and depressed.

You probably are trying to diagnose me, aren't you? Just kidding; I know I deal with some of the clinically diagnosed symptoms' listed in this chapter and even though I can read them or relate to them, just like it says, at times I still go through stages of ups and downs or feeling crazy, I will prevail in the end, hey I'm optimistic! Hopefully you are starting to understand me and others who have been through these issues...

CHAPTER 11

2009 BRINGS TWO MORE NEAR DEATH EXPERIENCES

The girls and I are pretty much settled in. We first stayed with Mignon, my Son-in-law Raymond and my three Grandsons for a couple of months. It was nice of them to let us stay there until we got our apartment in December. We are loving our new apartment; the girls also love their new school. Things seem to be going quite well for us. I'm still working at the seafood restaurant for some extra money and also have taken a part-time position as a poker tournament Director. Texas holdem poker is big these days and Georgia has poker leagues with over 40,000+ members, me being one of them. I have always loved playing cards and especially poker. I come from a family who played at all the family gatherings and as a child you couldn't wait to get old enough to play. My Granddad and Stepdad were avid poker players who taught us how to play and we always had fun playing with them.

One day while at work in the restaurant I had a crying spell. It was a Friday night, one of the most busiest days for the restaurant. I started crying for no reason and could not control it. I keep trying to go in the restroom between talking to guests to get myself together. I try to keep on my reading glasses to camouflage my red eyes but when I cry my nose also turns red, great now I look like I've been crying anyway, I sob even more then. I go back out there and try again then I go to the kitchen trying not to cry. Workers and Managers are now asking me what's wrong. I say nothing but now I'm frustrated with the fact I am crying over literally nothing, which makes me cry more. Oh Brother this is so out of control! I step into the General Manager's office and close the door behind me, he says what's wrong, I say nothing, just give me a moment. He says great everyone is always saying I made someone cry; now they're going to think I made you cry. I'm shaking my head no; I'll be okay in a moment. In the meantime one of my female Managers is assisting me with my guests so there is no lag time in our service to them. I leave out of the GM's office but am still in the kitchen area of Red Lobster; then to my surprise, another female Manager who I didn't think really cared for me came up to inquire if I was alright. I said yes I'm fine, she said no you're not. She then told me she's had these kinds of crying spells herself and she understood. She said when she's like that sometimes she goes and stands in the walk-in refrigerator in the restaurants' kitchen, she said the cold helps her to calm down and stop crying. She suggested that I try that so I go and stand in the frig; I feel quite silly and even more so when employees come in and out to get food items. I eventually come out and I'm not sure if I went home early that night or toughed it out but I am thankful for the compassion shown to me by those to female Managers. I absolutely hate crying spells!

In April I speak at the University of Georgia in Athens, for the "Take back the night" Rally and March; a demonstration against sexual assault held at Universities across the country during sexual assault awareness month which is held in April. We set up an information table for HUMS at the event. On Easter I'm invited to speak and tell my story at a church in the metro Atlanta area.

In May, 2009 I decided to leave the restaurant, it was starting to be too stressful for me. Also in May I heard "go in and possess the land" I jot this down in one of my notebooks. I don't know when or how this will come about but I will wait on the Lord to instruct me further.

The first half of the year was great then came the week of June 10/11. I have a meeting with a few people who want to volunteer with HUMS. I say as we are nearing the end of our meeting, you know I think I'm going to be ok this year when that date comes. I'm feeling like I can make it through without any issues. Then the 9th comes, anxiety comes too and all that it brings with it. I cry and cry. I call my oldest Daughter who had recently not spoken to me because of a misunderstanding in the family. She normally was not answering my calls but this day she picks up. I tell her I'm so mad that I can't control my feelings and that I get so sad around this date when I should be happy. I thought I has going to be okay this year I say. I pour out my heartfelt feelings to her and she consoles me. I tell her I'm surprised you answered your phone and she says the Holy Spirit lead her to answer. Thanks Holy Spirit. God is always looking out for us in so many ways. She suggests that every year around that date that I already have something planned. She knows I like to travel so she said already have a getaway planned where I engage in doing something fun and also something that will keep me busy. I think that's a good idea.

July rolls around and my Daughter number four, Jasmyn is turning seventeen! I decide to take her and my youngest baby, Kayla who is going on sixteen to the beach in Florida for her birthday. They had never been to Florida and we all thought that sounded like a fun filled weekend. The birthday girl was a little apprehensive about the ocean but I told her she'd be alright. The two of them spent most of the summer at the pool and had become good at swimming. I had tried on many occasions to teach them but now they finally embraced it on their own. So with what they'd learned, I reassured my soon to be seventeen year old that she would be okay. She had swam when we were in Mexico, with assistance from me and her other Sisters, in the Caribbean Sea when she was much younger but I guess she didn't remember that. She sometimes is prone to worry.

It's about a five and a half hour drive. We get there that night and check into our hotel. The following day, it's a rain storm so we still head to the beach hoping it will stop soon. It lets up a little; we get out of the car and decide to pick seashells (girly thing) and explore the beach. We don't go swimming that day the weather is too unstable. The next day it is a beautiful bright hot sunny day! We join the many others that adorn the beach. The girls and I are having loads of fun! The birthday girl is comfortable in the ocean and we do as the other families are doing which is; wait for the wave to come in, pick you up and place you closer into the beach. It feels like you're on a ride at the amusement park. I'd tease the girls saying "I'm going out into the ocean and I'm never coming back" they'd say "we'll save you" I'd say "no, it's to late" as I walked out until the water was up to my neck. Realistically as I looked out over that water, thoughts of a peaceful place popped in my head. One with no more worries…disappear into all that vastness. You know; stupid thoughts. We continued to play and have fun; here comes another nice sized wave, weeeeeee, and another…but hold on, this wave carries me out further in the ocean instead of towards the beach! My feet are not touching the ground anymore. Okay I don't want to be in the dark ocean where you cannot see the bottom or anything else in the water for that matter and not being able to touch the bottom is definitely not what I want either. Okay don't panic, its cool, just swim back towards the beach, no problem. Okay I'm swimming but not getting anywhere, what's going on, try again, still not touching the ground. I'm not that far out, what's going on…I try and try to no avail. Now panic sets in, I think what if one of those big waves comes in again, I've got my back turned and am facing towards the beach and can't see the waves coming; if it goes over my head, I could tumble under water and I read that when that happens, many people think they are swimming back up towards the surface but instead they are swimming down deeper in the water. They have become disoriented. Oh God I don't want that to happen to me…try swimming harder before one of those big waves come again, nothing; am I in the twilight zone? I look at the Lifeguards, they seem so far away, I try again, what's going on, I can't understand why I'm not getting anywhere. This water is so black there could be anything swimming by me…like a shark or God only knows what else! Focus, try again. Okay, okay I'm getting tired; maybe if I back stroke, no, still the same. It's like there is an invisible wall or barrier I can't get through. Maybe if I can get my Daughter to grab my finger tips maybe she could pull me in. I can't be that far from touching the bottom…Jasmyn, Jasmyn I need help! Hahaha, mommy you're so funny. NO Jasmyn I really need help! She tells me later that she

113

saw the fear in my face then, and for some reason I looked like her Granddaddy...she edges out to where the water is up to her neck, she reaches my finger tips then she says, my feet are barely touching the ground now...I panic and start screaming for help, I know that my Daughter just learned to swim but only has swam in a pool, never an ocean. I know she is not a good enough swimmer for this. My Mother instincts kick in; I definitely don't want my baby drowning. As I am screaming so is my Daughter, "help my Mom" she screams. To my surprise the Lifeguards get to us quickly, so does others that are in the water. I just want to feel the bottom; I just want to feel the bottom; I say hysterically! They hand me that board and I'm holding on for dear life, don't let go please don't let go! They pull me up to the beach. As I'm walking out of the water I notice that my whole body is aching. I guess I didn't realize just how hard I was trying to swim out of whatever I was caught in. Me and the girls jumped in the car, it took a minute before I could calm down and drive then I took my butt back to Georgia! Jasmyn said when they came to help me, they rushed by her but luckily someone pushed her further into a safer position in the water. I told her I didn't know that, I thought they were helping her too. I guess because she said help my Mom, they thought she was alright. It would take over a week before all my muscles would stop aching from the exertive and exhaustive work they did that day. I later found out from some Floridians that I was caught in a rip current or riptide and the only way to get out of one is to swim the way the current is taking you until the riptide ends, well this means you could end up miles down the ocean at a much further distance along the beach or taken out further into the deep dark ocean! I also learned that most people who drown at the beach die from being caught in a rip current/tide because they become exhausted and can't swim any longer. If I ever go swimming again it will only be in the Caribbean Sea were you can see clearly if the water is doing something crazy like that and you can see what's around you; unlike the dark, dark ocean! I once again experienced flashbacks, this time of almost drowning and I would jump up and try to catch my breath. That would go on for awhile. Many months later I went to an exercise gym and spa with two of my Daughters, after the workout we hit the spa area.

When I got in the pool, I got all panicky; it brought back memories of the ocean. I didn't think that was going to happen just by going in a pool! I love the water, if I did this in a pool then how am I going to go snorkeling in the Caribbean Sea; I love to snorkel. No need stressing about it, perhaps when and if that time comes, I'll be alright. Anyway thank you God again for saving my life and sorry for my thoughts out there...

I had started attending a new church that I felt was where God now lead me to serve. I told my other Pastors and also told them I loved them and appreciated them. I knew my new Pastor from his days of being an Actor and he and I worked on a popular production together. He has an awesome and anointed voice. He is also good friends with one of my best friend's Paul. Paul is the one who told me that this young man had a church in the Atlanta area and when I checked out the website I felt that is where I'm supposed to be worshipping and serving in this season. I also told my Son-in-law that I felt he and his family are supposed to be there too. I say to myself, this seems like a good ministry, its good word, I felt a great move of the Holy Spirit at times, the praise and worship is definitely great and they speak of reaching out to help the needy. I've been attending for about six or seven months now.

Well I ended up having to move in August even though I didn't want too. This is also a time when I reached out to my church home and they said they'd help so that we would not have to move. Then at the very last minute I don't hear from them. I contact our Pastor via text and he tells me that several people said that I said something that I had never said. He told me he'd call me back. He never called nor did anyone else. I was shocked that lies were told and that my church home never called me to see if the girls and I were okay; did we have a place to go, did we need food etc. One very kind friend I met in Georgia named CJ helped us move and he did a lot of the heavy things all by himself. I was blown away with the actions of my church. This church preached going out to feed the hungry, one day buying homes to place families who needed a home in them and doing other outreach ministries. Here was a family in the church hurting and in my eyes; they turned their backs on us. I was an active member and helped and sat with the ministry staff during service and attended the Minister's training classes. My two girls helped out with a couple of the helps ministries as well. I thought, even if we were not active members, it was wrong the way things were handled. I talk to only a few of my close friends who are also in ministry; I share my extreme disappointment and disbelief with them. I tell one friend in particular that I really want to write a letter to the church expressing my concerns and feelings on the matter. I say, I will never go back there! He says maybe you should write the letter.

The girls and I stay at a motel for about a month while I save some money up to move again. I am so depressed and I don't want the girls to see me sad but I'm in this little room with all my belongings, two teens and a dog; I'm sure they knew. I can't believe I'm back in a motel room again; I liked my apartment and was finally in a home after not really having a permanent home for so long. My friend would ask me via phone or text; did you write that letter. Not yet I'd say. He asked me that almost every week for the next couple of months.

My Cousin who lives in Stone Mountain Georgia, tells me she and her partner are buying a new home and she wants to rent her present home out. She said she'd rather rent it to family because she knows they will take better care of her home. She tells me that the girls and I can move in with them while they are waiting on their closing. She, her partner and her Son were very kind and welcoming to us in their home. She knew that I wanted to keep the girls in the high school they currently attended because it was an excellent school district; and that I really liked Gwinnett County better. I told her I really didn't know what to do but we do need a place to stay and she had a spacious and lovely place. She understood that and we moved in with her family on Labor Day. I loved her home but was inwardly torn about some things. The first was I have a really big spider phobia and Georgia has some really big and crazy looking and acting spiders! The girls are scared of spiders too, in fact most of the women in my family are; the exception that I know of is my oldest Sister and my Cousin. Her house was surrounded by trees, she loved the trees, but I never liked trees close to my home because spiders always come down out of the trees at night and because of that I don't like walking under trees at night and it was very dimly light so you couldn't really tell if one was there or not. I know that those of you reading this that do not have a spider phobia won't get what I'm saying but those who are afraid of spiders will! I didn't mind the 45 minute ride, the extra gas, the Georgia traffic etc. to take the girls to their school in Gwinnett County. I was willing to do this because I preferred that school so that didn't bother me. The only other thing that concerned me was the other areas of Stone Mountain. She lived in a nice safe subdivision but let's say when I would have to stop and get gas, there would be a lot of men mostly black; hanging at the gas station some times asking for money. That made me very nervous and uncomfortable. Now some people may take this the wrong way and get mad but please really hear what I'm saying from a survivor of a horrific crime's point of view. I don't feel comfortable or safe in a majority black urban type community. Remember the man who tried to take my life was black and from the hood. I feel safer in a suburban type diverse community. When I am in a majority black neighborhood or "hood", my guards go way up, I feel very paranoid, and I think I'm going to be attacked again. In my mind I say if anyone tries to touch me or if I think they want to hurt me then I'm going to go crazy on them! I am going to use every self defense move I ever learned and then I will probably run them over with my car on top of it all just to make sure no one hurts me again. They may have just been trying to ask for directions and I over reacted; I don't want to be that kind of walking time bomb but it's what I think I would do. This was the major reason I really had hoped to stay in the area I previously had moved from. Oh, and maybe the thing with her Son catching a poisonous snake in the backyard when he was a couple of years younger sort of bothered me but not because you'd every catch me outside too often, (spiders, bugs etc.) but because of Snow having to do his business outside. I love my Cousin and family and they showed us so much love while we were residing with them. I feel torn with my inner feelings and with wanting to show my appreciation of their kindness by renting their home even though I'm not really sure what to do.

"Did you write that letter yet" I think to myself no I didn't write it yet, I'm going to, there is to much going on right now,. I'm just going to politely avoid Will's texts and calls for now because I know he's going to say…Did you write that letter yet.

My Mom is moving to Georgia, yea! I'm very glad about this, I love my Mommy and I'm glad she's coming here! She recently told me that when I was a little girl I would say I want to be just like my Mommy as I watched her dress in beautiful evening gowns and gorgeous shoes as she prepared to go perform. She was an awesome singer with a jazzy style voice. Singing professionally at various venues. She still has a great voice and cool jazzy way of singing. She also sang at church often and received requests from people to grace them with a wonderful rendition. I did not get the singing voice but my talent bloomed in acting and other creative gifts but I still look up to my Mom who inspires me! Relating to my plight in this book, she once told me after along time had passed; that she was always afraid that Black would come to their house and hurt them after he got out of prison. Wow, you never really know what others who are affected by crime as the family of a victim, may be experiencing and wrestling with themselves.

I go to Michigan in September so that I can take all of my stuff out of those three storage units I had been paying on. Paying those monthly storage bills and trying to keep up my bills here is what got me behind in my rent. Here in Georgia, if you're seven days late on your rent, you get an eviction notice. Unlike Michigan, you can get two or three months behind then go to court and get ten or more additional days to either come up with your rent or move.

Just before I leave Georgia I go by my oldest Daughter's house to say goodbye to the boys. They all have the flu. I kiss them against Mignon's protest, saying these are my grand babies, look at those little faces, I'm going to kiss them anyway. Low and behold as I am driving to Michigan I am also now coming down with the flu. What we do in the name of love. I had planned to only have the girls out of school for a week and had got their school work in advance to cover that week. We ended up being there for three weeks, it took a week to even feel well enough to do anything.

I asked my Sister and mom if I can do a massive yard sale in their yard. They say yes, but what none of us were prepared for was the mass amount of my personal and professional belongings. It would take all week to get everything; it would fill up her whole two car garage, long driveway, whole front yard and porch. It required several days of loading and unloading a twenty four foot truck and utilizing several different crews of volunteer helpers whom I could only give a little money to for their services which if I had the extra money it would have been way much more in compensation. We get a permit, put ads on Craigslist, and other internet sites, put up signs etc. and in between adding more stuff we'd sale items. My Mother and Sister were having a moving sale too.

It was all so overwhelming, trying to get completely over the flu, so much stuff that no matter how much I sold, threw away or gave away, it still seemed like a WHOLE LOT of more stuff still left! To make matters worse, Snow gets deathly sick, he won't eat or drink and he doesn't want to go outside. I take him to the Vet and they say they can't find anything from a physical exam; they need to do an x-ray and blood work and so on. I do not have the money for that so I take Snow and leave. I slept in my car with my dog for several nights praying to God to make him better and to please not let him die. Ironically I had found my book on American Eskimo's a few days earlier and was proudly boosting how they are one of the most intelligent dogs and that they are loyal and loving. Then I flip the page and it says they usually live fifteen years...FIFTEEN YEARS! How old is Snow? Probably around fourteen or fifteen I think? Oh no. Then a couple of days later he is so ill like he is dying. So I stay in that car with my faithful dog just like he always stayed right beside me. Week 3 and a lot is gone but there is still some things I had yet to go through in half of the garage and a few items downstairs. We are far past our scheduled date to depart so we just add what we can to my half of the truck. My Mother let me share the truck she had rented and I gave her some money towards it. One of the other reason's it was such a hard process is because remember I didn't pack any of my things, everyone else did the packing and moving for me at that time so nothing was labeled which meant I had to personally go through each bag, box or cart to view the contents; which was a long tedious procedure. I have to leave the rest at my Sister's house and I know she probably wanted to kill me, sorry LaShawn.

The road back to Georgia would prove to be yet another nightmare. We had problems with the tow dolly for my Mom's car several times which resulted in lost time. Each time we stopped my battery died; I had never had a problem with it before then. Later down the road the truck would lose speed so we contacted the company who then sent us to a place where we waited and waited all day for someone to meet us and service it. Finally after literally all day, the one location said it was fixed, we hit the road and the same issue. We are getting upset and frustrated with this company and their services. Now they say they will give us a new truck well we were not about to unload and reload the truck after the weeks of packing and loading we had just experienced. They say they will send a crew to do this. We wait almost all day again. When we finally make it to Georgia we are exhausted. A trip that is normally a twelve hour trip turns into a several days trip! Snow has gotten better since we made it back to Georgia, maybe he just doesn't like Michigan anymore either.

When I got back I decided I wanted to find a new hair Stylist, preferably someone like the young lady I had in Michigan who did a great job with my hair keeping it silky straight and full of body like I like it. I also decide I want to color my hair so I stop by this one shop and I inquire about coloring. I am directed to a woman in the back. I tell her I want something like a medium blond color but I have been dyeing my hair black for a while. She tells me she can do it and get the results I want. She says she is a hair color Specialist and that she teaches hair coloring techniques at a nearby university. I say great if you say it will be fine then I trust you and then I say its two people who we always trust there word, one is our Doctor and the other is our hair Technician, I say it with a smile. She tells me that she has this conditioner that she will put on my hair after the color that will instantly strengthen my hair from any weakness or stress from the color she does. She proceeds to color my hair, it comes out multi colored and unevenly colored. She then decides to bleach my hair; I ask her if that would be safe, she reiterated that the conditioner she will put on will strengthen my hair immediately. I say ok, in a "if you say so" tone. She bleached it and then it was three different shades. I said ok this is crazy; I could have gotten these kinds of results if I did it myself at home. She said she was going to put the color on to even out the tone. And this was the third time dyeing my hair in one sitting. I was there so long that my Mom and two Daughters that came with me had watched two or three DVDs that the Owner had put in the player. I asked her again if she was sure my hair was going to be ok. She repeated what she had said earlier. She proceeded to rinse, condition, flat iron and style my hair. It wasn't the color I asked for and it wasn't completely even but by now I was just thankful she was finished. After a few weeks I started noticing that I was adjusting my hair in the back a lot, thinking the wind was blowing it and that's why I was feeling like it wasn't falling right. Then one day my oldest Daughter said Mom your hair looks a lot shorter in the back. At that point I grabbed a mirror and lifted up the back of my hair and to my disbelief, my hair had fallen out! I was mad and upset. I went back to the salon and they told me that the woman who did my hair wasn't there anymore. I complained to the Owner, told him what she kept telling me and reminded him how long I had been there that day. He said well I'll give you a discount to get treatments. I said I am not paying you all anything else. He then said ok we'll do free protein treatments for five weeks. I asked is that going to help, will my hair stop falling out. He said yes. I also asked if they verified what their employees tell them about their credentials. He said yes, and led me to another woman in the back. She conditioned my hair. My hair continued at a rapid pace to fall out. I was devastated, I cried every time I look in the mirror. I now had to wear a wig. When I went back that very next week, there was yet another stylist and I was told she'd take good care of me. I complained again telling him to look at my hair; it is falling out like crazy! And every time I come back here you've got a new person you tell me to trust. These treatments are not stopping the breakage and damage to my hair. You said that the very first treatment would stop the breakage. He said it takes several treatments. I cried there in that shop. Each week my hair continued to fall out until I was left with less hair than a man's low hair cut. The Manager there said I have a pretty face I would look good with a short style. I informed him I grew my hair long because that's how I wanted it. I sought legal help but was told I'd probably get about 5000 dollars but no Attorney was willing to fight my case because it was not enough money for them. I have always maintained my hair and nails; those are a part of my image. I like to look a certain way professionally. And now I felt so self conscious about my hair. It is now over a year since that happened in 2009 and my hair has been growing at a very slow pace. It is still short. I wore a wig all the time until the very end of 2010 when I took my hair down and noticed it had finally grew enough to wear my own hair in a decent style.

Will called me and we talked extensively about the letter; he made several good points. One was that maybe God wanted to bring a lesson from this and if I don't write the letter then how would the Pastor really know how it affected me and how I viewed what happened. I assured him that I still intended to write the letter because I knew it was important too. I am not one who is afraid to express my concerns and even if the Pastor never responded to the letter, it would not have mattered. I was not looking for that unless he wanted too but I needed him to know how I felt about the injustice that transpired. We were on the same page with that but where we weren't was at Will's view on this, he felt I should return to the church because I told him when I joined that I felt lead to serve there and that I felt I was going to be a help in his ministry and that they were going to be a help in my ministry. That was true but I did not want to go back there! However, after a very long Godly wisdom filled conversation and feeling the conformation of the Holy Spirit, I agreed to go back and serve and to allow God to handle the situation as He saw fit. Another excellent point Will made was the decision maker for me as well, which was that if I did not go back the devil would have the victory in trying to stop what God had ordained in bringing the two of us together in ministry. I was not giving the enemy any chances to destroy what God was trying to do! So I finally wrote the letter; when I did it turned out to be at least 11 or 12 pages long and I felt such a weight lifted off me and such a peace when I finished it. I took it to church and asked the Secretary to give it to the Pastor. I gave it to her because he was not there that day. Then I visited the church the next Sunday and I felt very uncomfortable but I still went out of obedience. The next Sunday I was in attendance again and let me tell you it was hard to go there and sit knowing what happened. On that drive to church I was talking to God about going out of obedience and how hard it was to force myself to go and the enemy was fighting me all the way there. When I sat in service that day I felt the power of the Holy Spirit in service again, which was something I didn't think I'd feel there anymore. That gave me a peace about being back there. The next time I attended the Pastor called me over after service. As we stood in front of the pulpit he said I've been meaning to address your letter but I've been caught up with so many things; he went on to say he was sorry and that it was probably just an innocent misunderstanding on everyone's part. I said it does not matter now it's in the past, let's go forward with what we have to do for God. He agreed and told me to make sure they had my correct information on file so that I could be updated. By the grace of God and through my obedience so many doors opened for me and so many blessings started to flow my way not that this was the reason for me doing what I did but the fact that it was a result of spiritual maturity to look beyond my fleshly or human thoughts and trust in God in my spiritual walk.

One Sunday in November, I accompanied my Cousin to church. Her Pastor spoke on moving away from family. He explained what he meant by that. But I felt it was a message somehow directed at my situation. That next day I was riding with my Mom who is scared to drive in Georgia because most Georgian drivers are very aggressive. So when I can convince her, she'll drive very short distances from her home as long as I'm with her, this particular day we were going down this street and I looked down a side street and saw a for rent sign, now keep in mind I had planned to save my money up and decide if I was going to stay at my Cousin's when they moved into their new home after the new year or move back to the area I was living in. Either way I had not planned to do anything until after the holidays and new year. I had seen many for rent signs in the area and ignored them because of that. So that day I believe God directed me to look down that street. I asked my mom to turn around. Normally I wouldn't say anything to her while she's driving so she won't get nervous but something told me to tell her to turn around. I did and we went down that street and I said I like these condos. I took down the number and even though there were two other places on the same street for rent, I was drawn to this particular unit. I called about it knowing I only had a little money saved up and had just paid out some money on several obligations. The Owner was very nice and told us we can go in and see the condo. He instructed us to catch this guy who does work on a lot of the condos in the area, while he was on the street and have him let us in. We did, he was nice too. When we went in I immediately fell in love with the place, it was so nice and comfortable. I really was hoping I could move there. I decided I wasn't going to beg my Father in heaven about it. No please, please Father can I please, please move here! Instead I said Father only if it be your will, then let us move here. I will be content in what you do Lord. I spoke to the Owner and told him I really like the place. I also told him I didn't have the money to move right now. I would have it after the holidays I exclaimed. I told him I have a small dog, he said that's ok. Nevertheless I said you and your Wife pray about it and let me know what your decision is. I tried not to think about it the next day. Then he called and said my Wife and I did pray and we decided to rent it to you. I was so ecstatic! He even said we could move in now and not to worry about November's rent. He also said I can pay the deposit part after the holidays. I asked if I could always pay on the fifteenth of the month, it works out better for me that way. He said no problem. Again I say God is good! We moved in and have been happy here for over a year now.

I start selling Clear an internet product, in late October and start receiving lump sum payments in December. It is going great; it's like having my own Franchise. I can contract others to work under me and pay them a percentage for their services. I 'm making good money and I have negotiated with three major stores to set up manned display tables and sign people up with our product. One store chain has twelve locations that the District Manager oversees and he told me we can go to those stores too. Now I can send my independent Reps out so that they can work those locations and reach lots of potential customers. The DM tells me we can do that with them after the new year. The other two stores let us set up during the holidays.

Everything is going great, more and more blessings are happening for me. Then on December 10th 2009 I am on my way home and as I am driving I feel like I have a pebble in my boot or something in there that is aggravating my foot. I tell my Daughter as I am talking to her while driving with my blue tooth earpiece on for safety. When I get home I take off my boot and I ask my other Daughter who is home to check my boot to see if anything is in there. As I'm wondering why my left foot is numb; she says she doesn't see anything. I think that's weird and my Daughter on the phone says Momma that's not normal, you should go to the hospital. I say no way, I'm going upstairs and get on the internet and do some business. By the time I walk upstairs my whole left leg goes numb. Now I'm worried, that definitely is not normal. I tell her maybe she'd better come and get me and take me to the hospital. I thought maybe what is happening is related to my not taking my thyroid medicine for several months. When my last prescription refill ended I didn't have a way or the means to get it refilled because of not having any insurance. I know that it is a medication I must take or issues can occur, anything from minor symptoms like skin problems to major serious issues like organ failure or slipping into a coma or the worse death. That's what my Doctor in Michigan had told me during the time I had health insurance. Hopefully I'll be alright...

We get to Emory hospital and my blood pressure is super high while my heart rate is super low. My blood pressure has always been on the lower side which was normal for me but now it was sky high. The very handsome emergency room Doctor (to the ladies, had to throw "handsome" in there because he was) tells us he is going to admit me due to everything that is going on, he says it may be a stroke. Help, help is there a handsome Doctor in the house! Just kidding back to what happened. I end up staying five days as they do all types of tests and also try to get my blood pressure and heart rate stable. They also started my thyroid medication. This is my first visit to a Georgia hospital and I am impressed. Everyone is kind and they send in Specialists from different fields to talk about what I possibly could be experiencing even before they know what it is. They also do every kind of tests they can think of that is related to my symptoms.

The hospital sends in an outside Neurologist to see me and to be able to accurately read the CAT scan and MRI results once I have those tests. She is the only one who is indifferent and unfriendly. Upon her first initial visit to my room, she says "so you say you have numbness in your leg but we don't have a way of proving that's true right now" ok do I really want to be up in a hospital making up stuff lady when it's almost Christmas and I was trying to run a business! The answer is heck no, but I don't say this to her instead I tell her the emergency room Doctor was concerned because of all that's going on and because in my twenties I was told that I had a TIA. A transient ischemic attack (TIA) sometimes called a mini-stroke, is an episode in which a person has stroke-like symptoms for less than 24 hours. A TIA is often considered a warning sign that a true stroke may happen in the future if something is not done to prevent it.

My leg continued to feel totally numb like dead weight most of the time I was there. When the results from my MRI came in the very unfriendly Neurologist told me the test showed that I have had several TIA's and that is what I had this time she says. I say when did I have them, recently or over the years? What should I do? Is this very dangerous? Why did that happen and what does it mean? etc. She doesn't give me any concrete answers to my questions; she just leaves out with comments not pertaining to any of my concerns.

The nice resident Doctor tells me they want to do even more blood work to try and figure out why at my age did this happen. They tell me I can be released the next day and that I need physical therapy at home, which they set up. They also tell me that I need to follow up with that same Neurologist because when they call an outside expert then the patient automatically gets a free out patient visit with that Specialist. Yippee, I'm so excited to follow up with her, NOT.

I ask can I travel to Ohio, my middle Daughter is graduating with her degree in CSI, criminal science investigation and I was going to also go visit my family in Michigan and attend my only Granddaughter's first birthday. He said no, if I ride in a car for a long period, a blood clot could develop because of my having the TIA. This saddens me, I was looking forward to going to see Alicia graduate and to seeing my family especially my Grand baby that I hadn't seen too often since she's been born and my five year old Grandson too.

My Mom and Mignon take the drive up there as I'm at home trying to recuperate. Speaking of driving, I try to drive myself home so I won't have to be a bother to anyone. Boy oh boy was that a mistake. My judgment of distance is way off due to the pain medicine I was still influenced by. I miraculously make it home but just before pulling into my driveway and garage, I decide to get the mail at our mailbox station. I proceed to do a turn to place me right in front of the boxes; as I am trying to do this I crash hard into the curb just in front of the mailboxes and a woman who I startled goes back up on her porch and stares at me. She doesn't come off until I leave the area. I think she thinks I'm drunk. I messed up my front end of my car, it was hanging down. Shoot!

The next few days I keep almost falling over to the left. A friend I met gives me his cane which helps me to keep some sort of balance. He along with Mignon and my other friend, CJ help me get the girls back and forth to school. Each day I am struggling more with my balance, it is worsening. On that Wednesday morning, three days after leaving the hospital, I try to get dressed to see the girls off to school. I shakily go to my walk in closet and fall over but I can't get back up. I'm struggling to find something to grab on to so that I could pull myself up. I just can't get up. I am thinking I cannot call the girls for help because I'm naked! So I keep trying as I am wrestling to get out of this short box that I fell in. later I thought that had to look comical, but at the time there was nothing funny about it! When I make it out I decide to call for someone to take me to the hospital. Mignon and my Mother had left the night before and were still driving to Michigan to go to Alicia and my Cousin's graduation. So I called CJ. He came and took me; when we got there I informed them that I was just released that Sunday. They take me to the back to wait for the Doctor. As I am waiting a hospital staff member comes in for me to sign some papers. As I'm writing with my left hand I look at the way I wrote my signature and it is not in my normal hand writing. I am tripping out and I start to cry because I don't know why I'm not writing the same. The heart monitor starts beeping loudly because I'm stressing and it's reflecting that through my heartbeats. CJ and the Nurse try to get me not to worry. So I close my eyes, I say CJ will you look in my purse and hand me my lip gloss, my lips are feeling chapped. He hands it to me I take it and close my eyes again; I unscrew it and hold the wand to what I think is the distance my lips should be to the wand. I wonder why I'm not feeling the wands' sponge brush yet. I open my eyes and my hand is way far from my mouth. I cry hysterically again, what is going on? I can't even Judge the distance to where my mouth is!

I call Mignon while she's on the road to tell her what's going on thinking she is the oldest child and she should know; to my surprise she burst out into tears saying I am turning around, I shouldn't have left you! She is sobbing so hard and Mom is asking her what's wrong. I feel bad and don't want her to worry about me. I tell her no please don't turn around, I'll be ok, Alicia needs one of us there.

Represent me by going. She still insists on coming back but I finally convinced her not too.

The Doctor does his tests and then he tells me I did not have another TIA, it is just the residuals from the same one I had. I ask why don't you all tell people that this can happen. He says because then people will worry. I said well this scared me not knowing so I still ended up worrying. After a few days I can write back normal again but I still had shaky balance and some numbness.

While I am recuperating I don't have much energy even when trying to call the girls for something. Snow stays in my room with me. Then Snow started doing something he had never done before. When I would try to call the girls in my weak voice, he would stand in front of my bedroom door and bark until someone came. It was like he knew to call them for me because I was sick. He is an amazing creature of God's.

My two babies at home really look after their Mom! Jasmyn is my Nutritionist and feeds me; Kayla is my Nurse and gives me my meds.

God gives me two visions for going into 2010 that I keep in my heart...

2010 Summarized...

I spend most of the first part of the year doing physical therapy in my home and recuperating. I still continue to get extremely tired, have double vision and get off balance some times. This is the case even up to the end of 2010 and finishing this book.

I think about getting social security just to cover the many tests and trips to various Doctors and Specialists especially since they turned me down for Medicaid. Sadly so many people suffer medically because of not having medical insurance. I think if those people who fight our President on this matter, could experience what it is like for them or someone they love, not to be able to afford medical help when they need it and if they felt what it's like to have to

129

choose whether or not to seek help for serious conditions that could lead to death; maybe they'd be more compassionate. We know hospitals can't turn you down but when you go, then you're up to your neck in bills! Lots and lots of medical bills which in turn also ruins your credit.

Mignon drove me to all my appointments and to see the evil Doctor. She still didn't address my concerns thoroughly and when I left there I cried to my Daughter; I don't like her, she doesn't help me to understand what's going on. Mignon comforts me. When we first visited another clinic in Atlanta I spoke with a very kind and compassionate female Doctor who listened to me and gave me answers and arranged follow ups to my medical issues. Mignon said you like her don't you, I said with a big old smile yes! She said oh great now I have to drive you all the way downtown to see this Doctor. That's my Mignon, lol (laughing out loud). Despite that remark, she was happy I found someone I was comfortable with.

In February my middle Daughter Alicia moved to Georgia and moved in with us, yea! She loves it here too.

An opportunity comes up to do the Census so I take it. The only sad and disappointing thing is I start the week of my twenty four year old Daughter, Amber's graduation in Michigan and now I'll miss hers too. I keep missing my Daughters' monumental moments...

Luckily I end up being promoted to a Crew Leader Assistant which is good for me because I don't have to go out in the field and walk in the hot July Georgia weather. I work it for over a month get laid off for about a week and am blessed to be one of the few people they call back for another operation. This one is about two weeks and I do have to go out in the field. It is hard on me but we can work at our own pace and set our own hours as long as we get the work done. We're laid off again and I get called back for a third operation which last just over a week.

My only Daughter who wasn't here was Amber then she moved to Georgia in July with her family and so do two of my Sisters and

Nieces! Yippee! They love it here too. Now all my Daughters and Grandchildren are here!

Back to the Census, during the last days of my second Census operation, I do get ill and have chest pains for over doing it with the field work; hmm maybe it was the twenty seven apartment buildings with four floors each that I had tried to do in one day. Up and down four flights of stairs in the scorching heat. I ended up in the hospital for a couple of days and under went tests for my heart. The tests results were all good. Thank God I don't need anything else to go wrong health wise. I was surprised when they called me back with the third operation; I knew it was going to be a third one but because of my getting ill at the end of the second, I thought they weren't going to call me back. I guess I was a good hard worker.

Through out this year, I have to follow up with my medical care at a clinic for people with my same dilemma on insurance. It's located in Atlanta and I go to Grady hospital too, also a place for people with no insurance, low income or no income. At first I was concerned with the quality of care I'd receive but I found out that Grady has excellent Doctors who are from Emory too. I like Emory Doctors; that puts my mind at ease, but let me tell you, at both these locations you have to wait hours and hours to be seen. My record time of waiting is nine hours and about fifteen minutes just to see the Doctor for my scheduled appointment time!

Now that Alicia and Amber are here, they've been taking me to my appointments too. They also try to get me out of the house when they are worried about me. I have been so blessed by my five girls; each of them has played a significant role in my life. Thanks Rhonda's angels!

I've got to tell you this funny and crazy story. Amber accompanied me to Grady for my eye Specialist appointment. As we are sitting there among the crowd of people this lady sits next to Amber. She is eating some buffalo wings. Amber says to me Mom we've been here a long time I'm hungry and this lady chimes in as she leans over on Amber, you can have some of my wings she says. We say oh no thank you. She says they're good take one. No thanks we're going to get something later. We go back to talking among ourselves; then a little time passes. The same lady says whew those wings was too hot as she is holding a can of coke in her hand. I say that's why I couldn't order me wings because you'd definitely need a drink after that. She says I got a drink girl and it ain't soda, laughing she says if you know what I mean. Me and Amber say oh ok. Not knowing how to respond and not wanting to laugh out loud at the craziness going on next to us. Amber goes up to the desk in order to escape our present company and then I excuse myself. My Daughter says Ma didn't you see when her boyfriend poured the liquor in her soda can; he had it in his sleeve and leaned over and poured it from there. I said I saw his arm as he moved away from her direction but I thought he had some type of tube in his arm because all I saw was the round opening of something. We crack up laughing, the things I endure with no medical insurance! That was too crazy, who gets drunk at the Doctor's office? We were there about eight hours.

Prior to that episode, the Neurologist at Grady had me get the records and DVD of my MRI and bring them in. upon his viewing the information, he says you did not have a TIA, you had a stroke. A stroke really, wow that sucks. I could have died.

He wants to do more test including another MRI scheduled sometime this month so that a year has passed. He wants to see if there are any changes. He says if nothing changed he still may want to do a spinal tap to further rule out MS which is what he thinks based on my past history in my twenties, could be the case, but he says if it was MS then I have done exceptionally well, because no one can have that disease for over twenty something years and not have severe damage. That is precisely why I don't believe I have it! And no way am I getting a painful and dangerous spinal tap!

The Doctors and Specialists don't really know what's going on in regards to my health but it is ok, I am going to be just fine. I feel good other than those minor things I mentioned. Ok maybe that double vision thing isn't so minor but hey I'm good.

This year has been a strange year for me in the sense of my normal church attendance. I have not been in fellowship in a church setting but on a few occasions throughout 2010. That is rare for me because I believe in corporate fellowship which is an essential part of our Christian life. The bible talks about how on many occasion it was corporate prayer, praise or worship that brought about change orchestrated by God after hearing His people address Him on one accord. Plus I know that it is healthy for your personal growth to stay in fellowship with other believers. So having regular and consistent attendance in church is important in the body of Christ. Not to just go for the sake of saying "I go to church every Sunday", but to go with the intent to serve, grow spiritually, worship, praise, adore, love and revere an awesome God with other believers corporately. For many years I have consistently been in service several times a week, but this year it started out that I was recovering from the stroke then I ended up working Sundays for the Census then other Sundays I would over sleep or sometimes I'd just be to sad and depressed to go anywhere. Then the year was over...

CHAPTER 12

CONFESS YOUR FAULTS

ONE TO ANOTHER

James 5:13-16

13 Is any among you afflicted? let him pray. Is any merry? let him sing psalms.

14 Is any sick among you? let him call for the elders of the church; and let them pray over him, anointing him with oil in the name of the Lord:

15 And the prayer of faith shall save the sick, and the Lord shall raise him up; and if he have committed sins, they shall be forgiven him.

16 **Confess your faults one to another, and pray one for another, that ye may be healed.** The effectual fervent prayer of a righteous man availeth much.

These thoughts don't follow what was written in the previous chapter, they were actually written prior to those chapters. In fact this is where I started writing when I only had part of chapter one finished and nothing else wrote so keep that in mind.

It gets deep...

On October 21, 2010 I wrote:

My thoughts on yesterday... I Trust God to keep me, and protect me and not let anything happen to me or my family...Yet, I have a fear, a fear of failure, that if I try again to do the things I am called to do, that I will fail, I won't succeed. Sadly this is what I think...

How can I Trust God in one area and not the next...Is it because I know he saved my life so many times as an adult and as a child...and because I've seen His grace and His mercy...because I've felt His great and wonderful love?

My fear comes from within, I have tried so hard in my adult years to be a success on a constant level, oh I have experienced many, many short lived successes, but not on an ongoing basis.

Here I am at fifty with no real accomplishments...

My failures...

It's hard to write them because I have for so long tried to think positive, be optimistic... If I say or write them, does that make it true? Will I be giving in to my fears? Will it make me weak and more vulnerable?

A thought within a thought...

Am I being selfish or unappreciative? God saved my life from attempted murder, from rape, from drowning in a riptide, from dying from a stroke. And that's just within the last three years.

The battles I fight inwardly all stem from here, I should be thankful and happy and without complaint.

Yet, I have a great sadness...

One of my biggest hurts is loneliness. Sometimes I feel that God doesn't want me to be with anyone or even get too close to anyone, whether a boyfriend or just a friend. That friend could be male or female. Then I think it is because after I was almost murdered, I asked God to protect me from anyone who would hurt me or try to kill me...So I think, I can't be sad because perhaps He is doing just that...

Then I sometimes think I'm going crazy!! I also think that a lot of people feel like this every now and then but, they keep it a secret...Just like I do.

I look at the faces of man (people) and happiness only seems temporary. And why do people seem so fake? I've tried all my life to be a good friend and have been hurt so many times. People lie and they hurt you...

Does God get mad when we talk about people, His creation? I know that there are good people as well or that people can have a good and a bad side, it's just that I give my all as a friend and it hurts when someone misuses that friendship or ends our friendship for no reason.

I wonder if that's why my life feels so destined to be alone...protection from hurt...

I know that all my joy, my love, my peace, my protection; my whole life is in Yahshua, Christ Jesus...I am at peace with that. God is all we really need...I know He is the answer to all things. To everything in this universe, yet I feel guilty saying I'd like to have someone to share my thoughts, feelings, joys and just everything in life with.

God said "It is not good for man to be alone" and that is so true, so I seek, long for a companion, one who is true and sincere and will love me and cherish me and understand me...

I know that God is a kind and loving God who knows our every thought and prayer and is passionate to our cries of pain. And that He understands my feelings and is more than likely preparing me and my significant other so that we are right for each other. But sometimes it seems as though it takes such a long time. Yet also I think I don't want Him to be disappointed in me for not waiting on the Lord patiently...

Trying to stay in a sane place is very hard, it seems easier to just let go and get lost inside of your head...shut down.

I know I'm not crazy just very depressed sometimes. I do try to go into my cocoon, well giant seashell. It changed this year (2010). You see I used to want to just stay in my cocoon after June 10th /11th 2007 you know; attempted murder and rape...I figured I could stay there and once I healed, emerge as a beautiful butterfly! Now it's a giant seashell I hide in, forget coming out, it's safe in here...no one can hurt me.

Ok, ok I guess that may sound crazy but it really is just a way God designed our brains to protect us from various hurts, pains and sadness. It's a coping mechanism. Psychiatrists and Psychologists have names for this but God in His infinite wisdom and brilliance, designed us like this, so I would guess it's healthy. As long as you come out in a better state or healed state. Everybody needs a "happy place" they can take their minds too...yet mine are more "safe" places...

This psalm was added on 11/3/10 because I felt lead to put it here...

Psalm 4

1 Hear me when I call, O God of my righteousness: thou hast enlarged me when I was in distress; have mercy upon me, and hear my prayer.

2 O ye sons of men, how long will ye turn my glory into shame? how long will ye love vanity, and seek after leasing? Selah.

3 But know that the LORD hath set apart him that is Godly for himself: the LORD will hear when I call unto him.

4 Stand in awe, and sin not: commune with your own heart upon your bed, and be still. Selah.

5 Offer the sacrifices of righteousness, and put your trust in the LORD.

6 There be many that say, Who will shew us any good? LORD, lift thou up the light of thy countenance upon us.

7 Thou hast put gladness in my heart, more than in the time that their corn and their wine increased.

8 I will both lay me down in peace, and sleep: for thou, LORD, only makest me dwell in safety.

Now back to my thoughts on that day, and yes another thought hits me...

I know that I am going to have to publish this in my book, hmmm that makes me wonder if people really will think I'm crazy or I don't have it together...you probably wonder why that bothers me so much. Well I have always tried to encourage, uplift and bring hope to people. I have always been seen as a strong person and I don't want people to lose hope. I am not saying that I'm all that, what I am saying is I know that when people look up to you and you let them down intentionally or not, it can sometimes have a devastating effect on them...look at my attacker Black, in his mind he was let down or hurt and he lashed out and tried to kill me and according to him, also kill himself. It doesn't mean everyone will be this extreme...

As I ponder these thoughts, God reminds me that I have a mission to write this book and to share my healing journey...

You know what's funny, when I started writing today I was simply writing my thoughts and feelings down. I did it only because when I went to Cherokee, North Carolina on Sunday 10/17/10 I was sad and depressed and decided I would go and play poker at the casino. Bad choice, I loss a lot of money, that made me more depressed! On my way there as I was packing, I put a brand new red spiral notebook in my bag. I thought, ok God you must have something you want me to write down. I didn't end up writing anything while in Cherokee but, as I was coming home, one of my best friends, Monica called me several times and so did others but I wouldn't answer. I was on shut down mode. Shutting down from people. People hurt you was my inner thoughts. After several calls from her, I decided to text her saying I love you; I'm ok, just very depressed, keeping to myself, on shut down mode. She responded back with an I love you too, praying for you and...I hear the Holy Spirit saying "write" ...oh great, so that's why the notebook. Now as I'm driving through the smoky mountains I'm thinking, I don't want to write! I don't feel like writing anything else for my book right now, I am not feeling inspired! Just very sad lonely and DEPRESSED!!! But I'm also thinking I'm not going to disobey the Holy Spirit either. So I get home and still not feeling motivated, I don't write. A few days pass, I look at that red spiral notebook, still no motivation. Finally after days of trying to stay in bed and sleep, by the way that was hard to do, I still have insomnia so my sleeping patterns are way off, usually I'm up all night then I try to make myself go to sleep but my mind is always going and going and going like the energizer bunny! Anyway so Thursday afternoon I get up, look at that red notebook, let my dog Snow out, attempt to eat which I don't really feel like doing, then oh great, I'm picking up the red notebook! So I think, ok I'll just journal my thoughts. My Therapist always said that's good therapy...just start writing, ok fine, here goes, what am I thinking, feeling...I think, I'll just do that, who knows maybe I'll feel better. Well surprise, surprise my writing is another passage in my book! Okay God I'm getting there slowly but surely...

Ok thought change again...

Disappointments...why does it hurt me so bad when people disappoint me, I think it upsets me more than most people. It makes me want to continue to stay in my shell...

I sometimes psycho-analyze myself (I studied psychology as a major and theatre as a minor in college) this is one of those times...

Why did I change from my safe place being in a cocoon to it being in a giant seashell?

My stages of wanting to stay in a cocoon held hope of emerging as a beautiful healed butterfly, yet my being in my seashell holds no hope of coming out, just staying in there where it's safe...perhaps that will change in time...

CHAPTER 13

HEALING, RESURRECTION

AND RESTORATION

Romans 12:2

And be not conformed to this world: but be ye transformed by the renewing of your mind, that ye may prove what is that good, and acceptable, and perfect, will of God.

Today is October 26 2010 and I have been soul searching all week. Last week I ordered an in home training course for Christian/crisis counseling so that I can become a Certified Christian Counselor. It covers the gamut from depression, anger management, anxiety, marriage problems, sexual assault or dysfunctions to heart matters etc covering thirty topics. I know this extensive training will empower me in my calling to help bring God's people into His presence for healing. I can utilize it in both areas of ministry, HUMS and Evangelism.

God has a way of bringing us back to ourselves like the prodigal Son where in the bible it says in **Luke 15:17** "and when he came to himself..." meaning came to his senses. That is the way I feel right now. I believe and know that God knew where I would be mentally at this time and He had me get that pamphlet in the mail which He knew I'd send off for and then start listening to the videos that remind me of who He is and also that those same videos would touch on some or all of the things that have been heavily on my mind. He knew that I would come to myself, and remember who He is and what He is capable of and who I am in Him!

When you come back to yourself, your true self, that spiritual side of who you are, you will once again experience peace like I have tonight. That peace that is spoken of in **Philippians 4:7** And the peace of God, which passeth all understanding, shall keep your hearts and minds through Christ Jesus. I love this verse; it is so rich like so many verses in the bible. Just before this verse are instructions to us. It says in **Philippians 4:6** Be careful for nothing; but in every thing by prayer and supplication with thanksgiving let your requests be made known unto God.

Then once we do that it tells us "the peace of God" not just regular peace but Supernatural peace that passes all understanding; we cant even began to comprehend that kind of peace, but its so calming, warm and loving...and then it goes on to say that this peace will KEEP our hearts and minds, two areas that need to be kept, shielded and protected. If you'll notice it doesn't end there, it goes on to say "through Christ Jesus" we cannot do it alone, we have to TRUST and depend on God.

But you may ask how do we stay there in that rest, that place of peace. Well the next verse tells us to think on things that are true, honest, just, lovely and of good report; it says if there be any virtue, and if there be any praise, think on these things. To me what encompasses all those things would be God, but any time you can take your mind to a place of happy thoughts then you are not focused on the negative or bad thoughts. Thus you can stay in a place of peace...simple, easy and true instructions right there in the Word!

I have known and understood this scripture for a long time yet I let my thoughts and matters of the heart over take me. Those thoughts were so loud and overwhelming that I allowed myself to succumb to them.

I forgot what God instructed me to do in those verses and in His instructions to "stay focused and cut negativity out of my life" funny that was aimed at Black back in June 2007 when I first heard it but God just reminded me, it's aimed at me now...

This book is written to help me heal and to help you who are reading it in whatever way God means to reach out to you. It is time for a "renewing of your mind" and for restoration. So again I say while you're reading search your soul, seek God's purpose for you through prayer, it's about you right now. Stop here and pray a **sincere** prayer from your heart.

Psalm 23:3

3 **He restoreth** my soul: he leadeth me in the paths of righteousness for his name's sake.

How do you and I make sure we stay where we need to be spiritually? Well for me I know that I have to play my gospel music periodically throughout the day. It keeps me in a place of adoration, worship and praise. When I'm there, it's no space for thoughts of my needs. For I know God knows them and will do what is the absolute best thing for me. Often times in my life He has done exceedingly and abundantly more than I had asked! Just as His word says in **Ephesians 3:20** Now unto him that is able to do exceeding abundantly above all that we ask or think, according to the power that worketh in us...

I also have to remind myself of His Word, so it's a good idea to find a particular scripture you like and memorize it, write it on the table of your heart, live it, breathe it! Whenever the enemy tries to come against you with those bad/negative thoughts, start quoting your learned scripture out loud so that you drown out the devil! Then rejoice! Sing, sing loud and dance a victorious dance! Hey it might sound silly but it works. Paraphrasing, the bible says David was so happy praising the Lord that he danced out of his clothes! He didn't care what people thought so you shouldn't either.

Prayer it is essential…

I talk to God and pray quick prayers for others or sometimes for myself, all throughout the day but I don't take the time to pray like I should. I'm working on that starting right now. I do always pray when I'm lead to pray for someone, but when it comes to me, I think that I feel like all is well already and that God is already in control of every aspect of my life and my family and love ones lives. Because I have already asked that of Him; that's whether I am happy or sad, I truly believe that with all my heart. Nevertheless I need to pray more…even in His word I know we are to pray without ceasing, for one another, for those in Authority, for the body of Christ etc.

Thank God often, He's is worthy of our thanks…

Another way to keep your mind and heart focused on positive or good thoughts is to "count your blessings" no really count them! Get a notepad and just start writing all the wonderful things that have happened to you. Even starting from when you were a child. Before you know it, you start thanking God for those blessing you had forgotten about! You will also find yourself in a joyous mode afterwards. Now that you've written them down, keep that notebook handy and when despair tries to creep in, grab that book and read those blessing and voila` you are back on the right track!

Seven key points for our spiritual well being:

- ➢ **MEDITATE ON HIS WORD**
- ➢ **TRUST GOD COMPLETELY**
- ➢ **PRAY MORE**
- ➢ **CONTINUOUSLY GIVE THANKS TO GOD**
- ➢ **WORSHIP HIM**
- ➢ **PRAISE HIM**
- ➢ **BLESS THE LORD**

THANK YOU GOD FOR THE RESURRECTION OF MY SOUL…

CHAPTER 14

STRENGTH AND TRUTH

My prayer for you and me is:

Ephesians 3:16-19

16 That he would grant you, according to the riches of his glory, to be strengthened with might by his Spirit in the inner man;

17 That Christ may dwell in your hearts by faith; that ye, being rooted and grounded in love,

18 May be able to comprehend with all saints what is the breadth, and length, and depth, and height;

19 And to know the love of Christ, which passeth knowledge, that ye might be filled with all the fulness of God.

Psalm 27:13, 14

13 I had fainted, unless I had believed to see the goodness of the LORD in the land of the living.

14 Wait on the LORD: be of good courage, and he shall strengthen thine heart: wait, I say, on the LORD.

Also Isaiah 40:28-31

28 Hast thou not known? hast thou not heard, that the everlasting God, the LORD, the Creator of the ends of the earth, fainteth not, neither is weary? there is no searching of his understanding.

29 He giveth power to the faint; and to them that have no might he increaseth strength.

30 Even the youths shall faint and be weary, and the young men shall utterly fall:

31 But they that wait upon the LORD shall renew their strength; they shall mount up with wings as eagles; they shall run, and not be weary; and they shall walk, and not faint.

The book cover depicts that last verse which is the vision God gave me when I sought Him on the subject. I sketched what I saw in my mind then painted it. What a beautiful picture of His glorious grace and mercy upon my life to allow me to be renewed so much so that I can soar with wings like an eagle!

So "WAIT" as in <u>serve</u> the Lord and as in <u>patience</u>, patiently wait on the Lord.

Nehemiah 8 and the end of verse **10** says **"for the joy of the Lord is your strength"**...

Our **strength** lies within the **LORD**, let us rejoice in Him, again going back to keeping our mind and heart focused on the right thing.

The world will tell you all kinds of ways to cope with life's issues; you know, all those "self" help books, CDs, videos etc. Well here is the problem, the world's coping mechanisms points to focusing on "SELF" when what we really need to do is focus on what God purposed for our lives.

I know personally just like you know or may sometimes feel that it isn't easy to not focus on ourselves, our needs, our wants, our desires etc. But where has it gotten us on a long term basis? As I stated earlier, I've had many short lived accomplishments that the world would look at and applaud. What I want is for God to look at my life actions and deeds and say "Well done".

I want to be seen in my heart as God see's me. Not because of me having "positive" thinking but because I learned to have "**TRUTH**" thinking! I'm not saying you shouldn't be a positive or optimistic person but let that come from the inner spiritual being in you that has an internal knowledge and understanding of the true you based on what God says about you.

I heard a wise man speak on the difference between positive thinking and TRUTH thinking, it made good sense so therefore, I'm sharing it with you in my own understanding.

The bible says in **john 10:9-11**

9 I am the door: by me if any man enter in, he shall be saved, and shall go in and out, and find pasture.

10 The thief (Enemy, Devil) cometh not, but for to steal, and to kill, and to destroy: I am come that they might have life, and that they might have it more abundantly.

Isn't that the "**truth**" the devil would desire to steal from us, that in itself covers a lot, like steal our joy, our family, our peace of mind, our hopes and dreams etc. and to kill, wow the enemy wants us dead and will go to any length to try and do this...even if it means getting someone to take their own life. Commit suicide, the cowards' way out. When I guarantee that if that person would have held on just a little while longer and learned how to just put his life into God's hands completely and learned that by seeking the "truth" about what God has to say about their life or that situation, the end results would have been victorious and all the things that put him/her in that mindset would have seen so trivial. To destroy us is another thing the devil wants to do. Completely destroy us in every way. Well thank God that His plan is different for us. God says that He came that we might have life and have it more abundantly! We can live a full, rich, prosperous and healthy life. I know that's what I want, how about you?

And then the next verse says...

11 I am the good shepherd: the good shepherd giveth his life for the sheep.

Isn't that such a wonderful loving thing our Lord has done for us!

Here is more awesome instructions to help protect us and keep us where we need to be.

Ephesians 6:10-20

10 Finally, my brethren, be strong in the Lord, and in the power of his might.

11 Put on the whole armour of God, that ye may be able to stand against the wiles of the devil.

12 For we wrestle not against flesh and blood, but against principalities, against powers, against the rulers of the darkness of this world, against spiritual wickedness in high places.

13 Wherefore take unto you the whole armour of God, that ye may be able to withstand in the evil day, and having done all, to stand.

14 Stand therefore, having your loins girt about with truth, and having on the breastplate of righteousness;

15 And your feet shod with the preparation of the gospel of peace;

16 Above all, taking the shield of faith, wherewith ye shall be able to quench all the fiery darts of the wicked.

17 And take the helmet of salvation, and the sword of the Spirit, which is the word of God:

18 Praying always with all prayer and supplication in the Spirit, and watching thereunto with all perseverance and supplication for all saints;

19 And for me, that utterance may be given unto me, that I may open my mouth boldly, to make known the mystery of the gospel,

20 For which I am an ambassador in bonds: that therein I may speak boldly, as I ought to speak.

I declare I will put on the whole armour of God and that I open my mouth BOLDLY in this book to make known the mystery of the gospel, I am an AMBASSADOR and I will speak boldly as I ought to speak!

CHAPTER 15

INWARD FEELINGS ON MURDER

11/03/10

I spoke to an old friend today, she told me that on June 20th 2009, Father's day her Husband was murdered...

My best friend Evangelist and Pastor Paul Burt's Son was murdered in June 2008...

The attempted murder on my life, June 2007...

I am saddened at the news of anyone who has been murdered; however I added this chapter because I realize that when people I know lose someone they love to murder, it really hurts me deep down in my soul. I am deeply saddened. It takes a while before I can feel ok.

I had to search myself and try to connect with my feelings on this issue. One of the things that flows through my mind is the thought that I am here by the grace of God, but my family could be sharing the news of losing a loved one to murder just as my friends had to do. I ache for their loss and for their pain. I pray for their healing. I see the pain in their eyes or hear it in their voice. I sense that they are walking in a state of disbelief, shock, moving in a world that doesn't seem real at the moment, dreamlike state quietly shielded behind going through the motions of life; but I see what is in their eyes. I feel connected to my friends in an odd strange way as they are grieving their loss. Not like when you are supportive of your friend type of connection although I am, but in a spiritually underlying sense. An unknown familiarity to what is going on. It is

149

not my spirit that hurts but my humane side feels the sadness of that loss. My spirit knows that if they knew the Lord then they are with God now and God will Judge the injustice they suffered. This is true about God's judgment whether that loved one knew God or not. Rest assured the murderer(s) will get their just reward.

I felt lead to add my good friend Paul's thoughts...

If it wasn't for depending on Jesus Christ, the source of my strength, I couldn't have made it. My Son looked after me and checked on me often during the time I was going through my divorce. We were very close. It was particularly hard because of losing my Son and going through divorce at the same time, those were the two low points of my life.

My Son had backslid and then two weeks prior came back to God. God prepared me in a dream so I know I'll see him again.

I will summarize the dream Paul told me about. He wrote a passage on this in his book. The book is called "Why me Lord, Why me" by Paul Burt to order the book email Paul at pburt1058@yahoo.com

The dream...

Two friends appeared to Paul and said come on, we gotta take this trip; come on we gotta do this. This big oak tree appeared with this door in it. Paul asked where are we? They said we have to go in. Paul then said I trust you. He looked behind him and there was a long line of people there. Then when he went in his two friends were gone. And then he saw this casket in the middle of this big hollowed out tree. In the casket he saw himself. When he went out another door on the other side he saw satan who said he has these scales. On one side of the scales, satan showed him this small gift wrapped box. He said it was all the good he had done. Then on the other side of the scale were a whole lot of gift wrapped boxes all different sizes that were stacked high up. They weighed the scale down. The devil said these represent your sins and he started to laugh. Then Jesus appeared. Jesus looked up and put His hands together; a small drop fell from the sky and it appeared to be blood. It hit the scale on the side with all the good I had done and it drove the scale on the good side into the ground. Then Jesus said now welcome into the kingdom that has been prepared for you since the foundation of the world. Then Jesus put His arm around Paul and then it got real bright and they disappeared.

In the dream Paul represented his Son who was murdered. Paul said because of his relationship with God, God prepared him for his Son's departure and prepared his Son for his arrival.

Most people are not confident where they really whole heartedly trust God, he says. You have to trust God totally no matter where you are in your walk with God, you can't take it back (what happened) he added.

He mentioned surviving a bad car crash, stabbing and being shot; but God said no to his dying those times. We all die daily, it's hard words but it's true. He says.

How do we deal with the murder of a loved one? We first trust God to hold us up and keep us, to serve justice for us and most importantly we trust that if we believe that our loved one knew God, then just like in Paul's dream, Jesus' blood out weighed their sins and they are at peace in heaven with their heavenly Father and our Lord and Savior. And as Paul said you will see them again.

Please don't drive yourself crazy in trying to figure out or understand the "why" we can't comprehend the mind of murderers other than the fact that at that time they emitted pure evil. We all know where evil comes from. Most of all please don't turn from God; turn to Him for peace, guidance and strength. God is not to blame, He is not the enemy. Remember the word says in John 10:10, The thief (satan, devil, enemy) cometh not, but for to steal, and **to kill**, and to destroy: the rest of the verse tells you that God gives life. "I am come that they might have life, and that they might have it more abundantly."

You may be wondering why some lives are spared such as in my case. Well I believe that the assignments that God ordained for me and other survivors have not yet been accomplished. We have a work to do for Him in this earth that must be fulfilled. It does not make us more special or better than the loved one you may have lost, it simply means they already did what they were supposed to do in this earth , even if they were a child who just touched the lives of the people around them, they did what God needed them to do. God is smiling upon them as they dwell in His presences now. I pray this chapter helps someone who needs to hear this. Be at peace now.

CHAPTER 16

MORE THOUGHTS...

11/15/10

I asked God to give me a vision for the cover of this book...He did.

In these past 2 weeks I have experienced joy and peace about what God is doing. I even surprised myself with the fact that I don't mind typing as much as I thought I would. I know that there is a reason why I had to do this whole thing alone and that is because God needed me to be spiritually in tune with the Holy Spirit as I write and format this book.

I had a dream the other night...I was in a house with some other people. They were upstairs, I hear a knock at the screen door and it is Black. I immediately became frightened and started yelling for help as he was coming in the door. Some men ran down the stairs and subdued him as he was trying to get to me...I had not had a nightmare of Black in a very long time. I guess my writing accounts have opened up my mind to the place I had shut off and dissociated from. It's alright though, it did not set me back, I'm still moving forward.

I also reflected on how if I met someone who had anything similar to Black, a caution sign would pop up in my head. Similarities like his first name or the color of his last name, his birthday, high yellow with a bald head, physical muscular build, things he used to say or even ways he may have frightened me that night, etc. I don't know why it bothers me, I know that person is not Black but it does happen in my mind as weird as it may sound. I thought about it because yesterday someone told me that his birthday is July 27th...Black's same birthday. Even after three and a half years this still happens.

11/16/10

I finally decide to go backwards in the book and finish the chapter which tells in vivid details, the account of Black trying to take my life. I had consciously been trying to avoid going there. It shakes me up even more than I anticipated. I have spoken before thousands of people telling my story. What I usually do is give a more summarized version that paints the picture of that awful day.

I unknowingly dissociated myself from my story which allowed me to tell it as if I were sharing someone else's story. I did not know the term "dissociation" when I first did this; it is a term I learned later from my Therapist.

Remember dissociation-A separation of emotions, the separation of a group of usually connected mental processes such as emotion and understanding from the rest of the mind as a defense mechanism, can be a response to trauma and perhaps allows the mind to distance itself from experiences that are too much for the psyche to process at that time.

Like I said Doctor's can explain to us how this works but it is God's awesome design of us that makes the mind capable of doing this. He gives us a coping mechanism that protects us. Thank you Lord.

Dealing with that chapter of the book I now have to face so such of what went on in that room... things I saw, I said, he did...it is overwhelming, I can't dissociate because I have to recall it, it is not a shorter version. It is so much more detailed, I have to visualize it, it's feeling too real for me so I try to go as far as I can, then I have to stop. I say I'm sorry God I can't finish that part right now. I stop. My stomach is so twisted, I'm a little shaky. Whew that was a bit much. I go online and play some gospel music and also go online and play free poker to take my mind off things. I can't write any more right then, not even in other chapters. Hours later I write these thoughts hesitantly... I didn't realize it would affect me that much. I don't even want to think about it right now. Just writing this I'm back jittery inside....have not been to sleep as usual, its 10:11 am.

11/2010

The week of Thanksgiving Snow gets very ill and starts urinating blood. My funds are low but I am determined to get him to an animal hospital. I call my good friend Dee Dee who rescues dogs and she tells me of a veterinarian hospital that will work with you. Amber, Alicia and I rush him there. They think its kidney stones and they take him to the back to numb him and put a catheter in him as they send us home. The Doctor calls and says he needs to do surgery on Snow, it's not kidney stones but he has a hard matter in him the size of a man's fist. So the next day he has the surgery and it is a tumor they remove from his bladder. The Doctor phoned me during the middle of surgery to tell me this and then he asked me did I want to put Snow to sleep or have him remove the tumor, ok no thought on that question; the answer is NO I don't want him put to sleep! Do the surgery. He warned of all the complications but I don't care what could happen because I am faithful through prayer, to believe he is going to be alright. Snow is my gift from God, I trust him in God's hands. He's recovering fast and doing great!

On an even happier note, three cars full of three of our Michigan families came to Georgia to spend thanksgiving with all the family that now lives here. It was a wonderful blessed dinner; we surprised them and had the dinner all prepared and served at my home. They thought we were all going out to a restaurant. One day we also drove two car loads to Cherokee NC; a two and a half hour drives from my town. We had a great holiday week before they headed back to Michigan on that Sunday. I think my Sister LaShawn and her boys will be moving here soon, I hope she will; she is the only Sister who is left there. As they were getting in the cars to leave, her seven year old stayed a distance away, when his Mom called him he said he was staying and throw him his suitcase, I laughed at those words then he proceeded to run away while short little Shawn chased him!

155

I found out shortly after they had arrived that they really came to see me because they were worried about me and they thought I had MS (Multiple Sclerosis). I assured them that the Doctor is unsure of what's going on with me but he thinks it could be that even though other test results were negative. He still wants to do further testing but I'm believing God that this is not the case. I also reminded them that God had saved me from so many other things and that He is definitely on my side even now. Hopefully that put their minds at ease. That was such a loving, caring and very thoughtful gesture. It really touched my heart, I love you family!

12/01/10

One of my old real estate classmates called with good news! He says he is about to buy some apartment buildings in Michigan, Chicago and Georgia and he wants to work with HUMS in making them into safehomes and shelters with healing centers and counseling in house! Wow that's awesome news! He plans to come down before Christmas or right after the holidays to meet with me and his business connection here, I'm excited! GOD is GOOD!

12/07/10

Life issues that weigh on a survivor are like a scale that is hard to balance. I say this today because sometimes added things can over tip the scales! It is a very delicate balance. Picture this; the survivor is holding weights in both hands with out stretched arms. On one side she/he is balancing trying to maintain some type of normalcy and keeping themselves sane and on the other side of the scale trying to balance the everyday issues of life and keeping it together there. Then someone throws a new problem at you and WOW, oh shoot, keep it together, keep the balance, keep it, don't let your arms fall, even if they fell tired, ok how do he rebalance the scales, HELPPPP! Don't scream, ok you can do it just another challenge, don't quit, you're not going to tip over or fall off the edge, don't give up, don't faint, don't go insane, breathe, breathe... that's what it feels like.

12/14/10

By the way, I write in a peculiar way, I go back and forwards to different chapters as I am lead. I am actually almost finished. Thanks Lord.

I spoke with a new friend today; he is a Minister as well. He gave me a prophetic word; he gave a reference that a part of this verse is also a part of my ministry...

John 10:10

10 The thief cometh not, but for to steal, and to kill, and to destroy: I **am come that they might have life, and that they might have it more abundantly.**

Ironically I had already used this scripture several times throughout this book. I put the part he mentioned in bold print. He pointed out an awesome thing; not only did God come that we might have life but that we might also have life more abundantly. That's two-fold!

I also feel God gave me my life again that night and now because of that, I am experiencing life more abundantly too. I am truly blessed to be here.

As I read more in this biblical chapter, God brought me to this portion as well...

John 10:28-30

28 And I give unto them eternal life; and they shall never perish, neither shall any man pluck them out of my hand.

29 My Father, which gave them me, is greater than all; and no man is able to pluck them out of my Father's hand.

30 I and my Father are one.

God saved and protected me! We know that Jesus came that we might be saved but what hit me as I was reading this is God the

Father and our Lord who are one, did not allow this man to pluck me out of His hand. If you are a survivor too then He did not allow anyone to pluck you out of His hand either. Oh what love; To God be the glory!

We have life; now let us enjoy that life more abundantly...

A longer, richer and fuller life...

Abundantly in every sense of the word! Walk in your blessings!

God's thoughts...

Jeremiah 29:11

11 For I know the thoughts that I think toward you, saith the LORD, **thoughts of peace, and not of evil, to give you an expected end.**

It will end up being about three and a half years before I am finished with the majority of every chapter in this book. It is funny how God spiritually formatted and lead me as I wrote. When I first started writing I had planned to only mention Black in the opening pages; just a little about how we met that's it and then go into what happened that unfortunate night that almost led to my demise. Then when I picked it up again I was guided into revealing more about Black's background which if I would have written intensely in the beginning, would not be in here. Because at that time I could care less about Black and I didn't see the significance in going into any other details about him. But I believe God had to allow me to recover enough along my healing journey to hear Him; each time further down that road I'd say ok Lord I hear you, I need to add this in here... Even with those times I still only had written a part of chapter one and that was over a three year time period. It took me about three focused and dedicated months to write everything else, nineteen chapters and about 200 pages later I accomplished my goal and mission.

I was very ecstatic on New Year's eve because I completed each of the chapters I had to finish thus being done with that aspect of every chapter in my book and as I mentioned, reaching that goal. Now in January I have been reading the whole book in it's entirety to edit, check the flow of things, move some paragraphs around etc. and add a couple of things God put upon my heart to insert. The writings beyond this point but only in this "thoughts" chapter occur in January 2011...

Change...

Who can change someone else? No one but God can. You can influence their behavior but not change that person. We cannot physically change our whole being either; you can alter your outer appearance and some inward things of the body too but we are made of flesh and spirit so complete change would have to encompass both. God has also given us the ability to make our own decisions whether we choose right or wrong. So we can change a situation or physical aspect, but not the spiritual side without proper Godly wisdom and direction. If needed that's what we should strive for.

What does "change" mean, the definition says: to become different, or make something or somebody different, to exchange, substitute, or replace something, to remove something dirty or used and replace it with another that is clean or unused etc. When does change happen? Even when I saw myself in a cocoon a change would have to occur in order for me to become that butterfly, figuratively speaking. It happens when an effort or action is made in a different direction. Change cannot happen when one is still, not in movement whether it is in thought or deed. There are times when God will tell you to stand still. Like in Psalm 46:10 Be still, and know that I am God: I will be exalted among the heathen, I will be exalted in the earth. Then you know you have to do just that. I remember the first time I heard "hush, be still and know I am God" years ago at that time I didn't even know it was a scripture. But I halted what I was doing as I was instructed.

In order to heal there was to be movement in the appropriate direction. We can seek profession help in our healing and that is good, it will certainly assist in the process, but if we want total healing then we have to rely on a much higher power and that is

God. We can't sit still unless God tells us too. If He doesn't then we have to make progress by doing what it takes to go forward. It can be very tiny little itty bitty baby steps, as long as we are progressive. It could be in the form of mental, physical, emotion or spiritual advancement. In the eyes of a survivor, even those small accomplishments feel like monumental sized steps.

Hold on to God's hand and let him lead you forward, but remember in order for change to happen, you've got to make a move before you can advance. Keep heading down that straight road that God has you on just like the cover of this book.

Provision God's way...

The wonderful Landlord's God gave me, have been awesome and supportive to my needs in regards to my November and December rent. They allowed me to stay rent free those two months because of my funds being low from my letting my extra incomes go so that I could focus on this book. I was looking for financial provision to pay my rent but God had already worked it out with the Carter's. Thank you for your kindness.

I had a thought about how God gives me insight or visions for the new year and I thought hmm I didn't have a vision at the end of this year 2010 but God reminded me that he gave me insight and is preparing me...2011 is the year for increase in my ministry more than at any point in the history of my life. The Song "Open the flood gates of heaven, let it rain" has been particularly on my mind and when I went to church at my Atlanta church home recently, there was a banner that read "2011 is the year of abundant rain". The "increase" is not necessarily about finances, I believe it is about growth in many or perhaps in all the areas I currently have a vision to oversee in ministry. I believe it means the past visions and preparation coming into manifestation in this season. Revealing itself in the magnitude God showed me...every preordained aspect. My ministry taking off to higher heights through and in Christ Jesus!

When I was doing the actual painting of the book cover I felt so much anxiety and weird fear as I painted the figure of Black and as I attempted to capture the woman that reflects me. I guess because I was trying to make it look like him and because I was trying to bring out the fear I felt in the facial expression of my rendition. That brought about a real intensity of focused concentration in my mind that scratched at those memories. It was intense but it was not nearly as bad as writing chapter two. The other amazing thing was when I was painting what was supposed to be me with wings as an eagle; I saw the face of this woman before I painted it. She was there and I kept thinking this is not looking like me, it is like I am seeing a mixture of me with this woman, I feel like it is my guardian angel's face. That may sound really weird to some but if you do your biblical research there is mention of people having angels assigned to them. I added the original sketch I had done of the book cover on one of the last pages in this book because there are some things I want to point out. When I sketched me with wings I saw my face as I drew it and you can clearly see her soaring with eyes closed, smiling and at peace...the vision God gave me then. It was clear and flowed so easily as I drew what I was seeing and the funny part of my drawing the face on the soaring woman was even though it was just closed eyes and a smile, no real detailing, it looked like me when I finished. When my Daughter saw the sketch she said the same remark. However, when I painted the winged woman it turned out differently, I didn't really see me I saw a woman that exudes peace and power and it is like she is flying and some what hovering rather than soaring and her head kept looking in the direction of Black and me. I kept trying to do it like I first envisioned it. If you will notice the figures are pretty much like the picture I previously did but for some reason she was not turning out like that. Revelations flooded my mind with the why this figure is not coming out the way I first sketched it. For one thing, I knew her eyes had to be open because I saw it in the tan outlined face before I painted it. Look back at the cover, she's looking without fear in the direction of the darkness I endured, a representation of being in a place of peace to look back on that darkness and still be victorious in rising above it. When God gives you wings you won't only soar but you can and will rise above your situation and come out triumphant! I look at the winged woman and I smile broadly. The sun in both pictures was really supposed to be a brilliant white light that represented the magnificent glory of God which is what carried me throughout this healing journey, but I could not capture what I was seeing so I just made it a sun that represents God's glory.

As I ended my painting for that night that lead into just before 7 in the morning on Sunday, I get another revelation it is time to get back to my regular routine of attending church and serving! I asked God to wake me in enough time to get ready for noon service because I knew how tired I was and that I'd only be getting a few hours sleep. Why did my phone ring at ten something in the morning by the time I got to it I had missed the call, when I looked at the phone the number was from an unknown caller! Thanks for the wake up call God. 01/09/11 I went up after service that day and told Pastor Murphy what I heard that morning and that I was back and ready to serve he said good because I need you.

01/12/11 This is where I am in my mind...I'm floating in an open boat in the vast sea, looking up at God and waiting on Him...the sea is calm, I'm not hiding in anything...just waiting...

CHAPTER 17

MATTERS OF THE HEART

Renewing your spirit and getting your heart right!

We determine who we are by the condition of our hearts...

Proverbs 23

7 For as **he thinketh in his heart, so *is* he:** Eat and drink, saith he to thee; but his heart *is* not with thee.

Matthew 6

21 For where **your treasure is**, there will **your heart** be also.

Have you ever been so consumed by something that it is all you can focus on, talk about or think about. You carry it in your heart. I remember a wise man (Pastor Lane) ministering about what we carry in our hearts. At the time I was going through a divorce and was so frustrated with everything that was going on. Things were taking so long to happen, the courts kept postponing and my ex in this second marriage was being a jerk. The only thing I asked of him was to keep me on his insurance because I had to periodically get blood work and take medicine for the rest of my life after having my thyroid removed. He knew how serious this was but he wanted to fight me on this issue through the divorce court.

We didn't have any children together or property together so it should have been an easy quick and uncomplicated divorce. I had only been married to him for three and a half years. My first marriage was 20 years and the two of us were civil minded people so that was a quick procedure. In fact my first Husband didn't even

163

retain an Attorney and he also paid for half of my Attorney fees. Why was this man who was in ministry as well, being so difficult I'd ponder? So much was going on, it consumed my heart. Then once I heard that word, I stop **thinking** on those things and changed my focus to positive things. Things that lined up to what God was saying about my life. I felt so renewed in my spirit.

Psalm 51:10

Create in me a clean heart, O God; and **renew** a right spirit within **me**.

It does not say give us a "new" spirit; it says "renew" a "right" spirit. God already knows that we have a good spirit in us when it is the right spirit; after all He dwells in us too!

After that I felt great, I decided to **guard** my heart and only let good, constructive, positive and inspirational things in there. That brought about peace as well.

Proverbs 4:23

23 **Keep (guard) thy heart with all diligence; for out of it are the issues of life.**

The issues of life that comes out and how we act are directly tied to our condition of our hearts, the matters of our hearts causes us to react to what we hold inside of the heart. When there is so much negativity or heaviness, there is no room for peace and happiness. That negativity manifests itself and shows in our behavior relating to the issues of life.

Here is another biblical example:

Matthew 12:33-35

33 Either <u>make</u> the tree good, and his fruit good; or else make the tree corrupt, and his fruit corrupt: for the tree is known by his fruit.

34 O generation of vipers, how can ye, being evil, speak good things? **for out of the abundance of the heart the mouth speaketh.**

35 **A good man out of the good treasure of the heart bringeth forth good things:** and an evil man out of the evil treasure bringeth forth evil things.

What are you allowing in your heart right now search yourself, look deep within.

Mark 7:6, 18-23

6 He answered and said unto them, Well hath Esaias prophesied of you hypocrites, as it is written, This people honoureth me with their lips, **but their heart is far from me.**

18 And he saith unto them, Are ye so without understanding also? Do ye not perceive, that whatsoever thing from without entereth into the man, it cannot defile him;

19 **Because it entereth not into his heart**, but into the belly, and goeth out into the draught, purging all meats?

20 And he said, That which cometh out of the man, that defileth the man.

21 For from within, out **of the heart of men**, proceed evil thoughts, adulteries, fornications, murders,

22 Thefts, covetousness, wickedness, deceit, lasciviousness, an evil eye, blasphemy, pride, foolishness:

23 **All these evil things come from within, and defile the man.**

Most of us have good intentions but we have to look at our inner man, the very essences of who we are…any of us could so easily let those things that defile us come out. So it is essential that we learn how to keep our heart in the right condition so that we don't end up with a heart "attack" when you phrase it this way it helps to give a visual of how serious it is to keep the right things in our hearts in order to obtain a healthy heart and lifestyle.

What happens when you worry or are broken compared to what happens when a good word and merriness is in your heart!

Proverbs 12

25 Heaviness in the heart of man maketh it stoop: but a good word maketh it glad.

Proverbs 17

22 A merry heart doeth good *like* a medicine: but a broken spirit drieth the bones.

Proverbs 15

13 A merry heart maketh a cheerful countenance: but by sorrow of the heart the spirit is broken.

God loves you...

Psalms 147:3

He **healeth** the broken in heart, and bindeth up their wounds.

TRUST GOD...

Proverbs 3:5, 6

5 **Trust in the LORD with all thine heart; and lean not unto thine own understanding.**

6 In all thy ways **<u>acknowledge him</u>**, and **he shall direct thy paths.**

Don't look at the picture that is right in front of you; but look at it like this; it is just a part of the whole picture. It is just a part of the puzzle. See life, the picture of your life, like God sees it for you.

Trusting in the Lord and having a change of heart towards God as well will result in this…

Psalms 28:7

The LORD [is] my strength and my shield; **my heart trusted in him,** and I am helped: therefore **my heart greatly rejoiceth**; and with my Song will I praise him.

Psalm 19

7 The law of the LORD *is* perfect, **converting the soul**: the testimony of the LORD *is* sure, **making wise the simple.**

8 The statutes of the LORD *are* right, **rejoicing the heart**: the commandment of the LORD *is* pure, **enlightening the eyes.**

14 **Let the words of my mouth, and the meditation of my heart,** be acceptable in thy sight, O LORD, **my strength, and my redeemer.**

Psalm 40

8 **I delight to do thy will, O my God: yea, thy law** *is* **within my heart.**

Psalm 37

3 **Trust in the LORD, and do good;** *so* **shalt thou dwell in the land, and verily thou shalt be fed.**

4 **Delight thyself also in the LORD; and he shall give thee the desires of thine heart.**

5 **Commit thy way unto the LORD; trust also in him; and he shall bring** *it* **to pass.**

6 And he shall bring forth thy righteousness as the light, and thy judgment as the noonday.

I Kings 8

23 And he said, LORD God of Israel, *there is* no God like thee, in heaven above, or on earth beneath, who keepest covenant and mercy with **thy servants that walk before thee with all their heart:**

Psalms 139:23-24

Search me, O God, and know my heart: try me, and know my thoughts: And see if [there be any] wicked way in me, and lead me in the way everlasting.

Remember, the things in your heart become your focus, it not only takes up all the space in your heart but then it consumes your mind as well.

When we trust God we put away worry and doubt. We need to trust Him one hundred percent and rest in that place.

God knows what is really in our hearts!

Proverbs 24

12 If thou sayest, Behold, we knew it not; doth not **he that pondereth the heart consider** *it*? **and he that keepeth thy soul, doth** *not* **he know** *it*? **and shall** *not* **he render to** *every* **man according to his works?**

I Kings 8

39 Then hear thou in heaven thy dwelling place, and forgive, and do, and give to every man according to his ways, **whose heart thou knowest; (for thou,** *even* **thou only, knowest the hearts of all the children of men;)**

Ecclesiastes 11

9 Rejoice, O young man, in thy youth; and let thy heart cheer thee in the days of thy youth, and walk in the ways of thine heart, and in the sight of thine eyes: **but know thou, that for all these** *things* **God will bring thee into judgment.**

10 **Therefore remove sorrow from thy heart, and put away evil from thy flesh**: for childhood and youth *are* vanity.

Proverbs 16

1 **The preparations of the heart in man, and the answer of the tongue,** *is* **from the LORD.**

2 All the ways of a man *are* clean in **his own eyes**; but the LORD weigheth the spirits.

3 <u>Commit</u> thy works unto the LORD, and <u>thy thoughts shall be established.</u>

9 **A man's heart deviseth his way: but the LORD directeth his steps.**

Psalm 73

26 My flesh and my heart faileth: *but* **God** *is* **the strength of my heart, and my portion for ever.**

Jeremiah 17

9 The heart *is* deceitful above all *things*, and desperately wicked: who can know it?

10 **I the LORD search the heart,** *I* **try the reins, even to give every man according to his ways,** *and* **according to the fruit of his doings.**

God is greater than our heart...

I John 3

19 And hereby we know that we are of the truth, and shall assure our hearts before him.

20 **For if our heart condemn us, God is greater than our heart, and knoweth all things.**

21 **Beloved, if our heart condemn us not,** *then* **have we confidence toward God.**

22 **And whatsoever we ask, we receive of him, <u>because we keep his commandments, and do those things that are pleasing in his sight.</u>**

23 **And this is his commandment, That we should believe on the name of his Son Jesus Christ, and love one another, as he gave us commandment.**

24 And he that keepeth his commandments dwelleth in him, and he in him. And hereby we know that he abideth in us, by the Spirit which he hath given us.

Know this...

Proverbs 14:33

33 **Wisdom resteth in the heart of him that hath understanding**: but that which is in the midst of fools is made known.

Proverbs 15

14 **The heart of him that hath understanding seeketh knowledge**: but the mouth of fools feedeth on foolishness.

15 All the days of the afflicted *are* evil: **but he that is of a merry heart** *hath* **a continual feast.**

Proverbs 2

1 My Son, if thou wilt receive my words, and hide my commandments with thee;

2 **So that thou incline thine ear unto wisdom, and apply thine heart to understanding;**

3 Yea, if thou criest after knowledge, and liftest up thy voice for understanding;

4 If thou seekest her as silver, and searchest for her as for hid treasures;

5 Then shalt thou understand the fear of the LORD,and find the knowledge of God.

6 For **the LORD giveth wisdom**: out of his mouth cometh knowledge and understanding.

Take heed to this...

Proverbs 28

14 Happy *is* the man that feareth alway: **but he that hardeneth his heart shall fall into mischief.**

25 **He that is of a proud heart stirreth up strife**: but he that putteth his trust in the LORD shall be made fat.

26 **He that trusteth in his own heart is a fool:** but whoso **walketh wisely, he shall be delivered.**

God can also **revive** your spirit and heart...

Isaiah 57:15

For thus saith the high and lofty One that inhabiteth eternity, whose name [is] Holy; I dwell in the high and holy [place], with him also [that is] of a contrite and humble spirit, **to revive the spirit of the** humble, and to revive the heart of the contrite ones. (contrite, worn out, ground to pieces, feeling contrition; repentant)

Do this with all diligence...

Psalms 27

8 *When thou saidst,* Seek ye my face; **my heart said unto thee, Thy face, LORD, will I seek.**

14 Wait on the LORD: be of good courage, and **he shall strengthen thine heart: wait, I say, on the LORD.**

Have faith and know this with ALL YOUR HEART...

Hebrews 11:6

But without faith it is impossible to please him: for he that cometh to **God** must believe that **he is,** and that **he is a rewarder** of them that **diligently seek him.**

Be an example of a BELIEVER!

1 Timothy 4:12

[12]**Let no man despise thy youth; but be thou an example of the believers, in word, in conversation, in charity, in spirit, in faith, in purity.**

In 2008, God led me to do a two part series called "A Change of Heart" it goes more in depth on this subject. On occasion, I have to remind myself of the Godly wisdom pertaining to the heart too. This is for us and the body of Christ for our edification.

Even as I write this chapter, I am reminded of what is in my heart at this moment and I found it was consumed with how I was going to meet my monthly financial obligations. This included my rent which is due in two days. I stopped my other sources of making extra money to focus on finishing this book before 2010 is out, as I know God instructed me to do; so deep down in my heart under all the other thoughts; is the knowledge that I know without a doubt that some way some how God will provide. And He did as I mentioned in another chapter!

I had to empty all those other things out and let the peace that only God can give, rest in my heart. Now on this next day I can work feeling renewed again. It is amazing to know that God will renew us over and over again...He is AMAZING!

Ephesians 3:14-19

14 For this cause I bow my knees unto the Father of our Lord Jesus Christ,

15 Of whom the whole family in heaven and earth is named,

16 That he would grant you, according to the riches of his glory, **to be strengthened with might by his Spirit in the inner man;**

17 **That Christ may dwell in your hearts by faith**; that ye, being rooted and grounded in love,

18 May be able to comprehend with all saints what is the breadth, and length, and depth, and height;

19 And to know the love of Christ, which passeth knowledge, **that ye might be filled with all the fulness of God.**

CHAPTER 18

MIND OF CHRIST

This was an assignment in one of my ministry classes then made into a sermon. It is one of my favorites; it is so rich in knowledge and Godly wisdom. When you fully understand and live it, you truly will be a humble servant of the most high God...

Philippians 2:5-11

5 Let this mind be in you, which was also in Christ Jesus:

6 Who, being in the form of God, thought it not robbery to be equal with God:

7 But made himself of no reputation, and took upon him the form of a servant, and was made in the likeness of men:

8 And being found in fashion as a man, he humbled himself, and became obedient unto death, even the death of the cross.

9 Wherefore God also hath highly exalted him, and given him a name which is above every name:

10 That at the name of Jesus every knee should bow, of things in heaven, and things in earth, and things under the earth;

11 And that every tongue should confess that Jesus Christ is Lord, to the glory of God the Father.

THE MINDSET OF CHRIST...

His word tells us that we should take upon us the mindset of Christ, and that is not to think more of ourselves but rather of what God has purposed for us in the earth. As well as to serve God and man in the way God would have us to do it, even as a bond slave would have, without murmuring or complaining. You may have many talents, skills, gifts, titles, status or prominent positions in life, but we are still to have the mentality of a true servant of God and realize material things or positions don't make the man, but it is the condition of the heart, the state of the mind and the willingness to serve God and others.

Jesus could have been anything on earth, a king, a nobleman, a ruler etc. because he is God, but because of the love He and our Father have for us, Jesus took upon him the form of a servant. I believe one of the reasons He did this is for an example to us. Verses 6 and 7 talk about Him being God and legally (not robbery) being equal with God and even though He was made in the likeness of men and people saw Him in the fashion of a man, He was still God. KENOSIS [keh NOE sis] is a theological term used in connection with the dual nature of Jesus as fully human and fully divine. The word comes from a Greek verb which means "to empty", He emptied Himself. Therefore we should have that same attitude. We should empty ourselves so that God can fill us with His pre-ordained purpose for our lives...putting "self" aside so that God can FULLY use you!

We also have to humble ourselves as well. Jesus chose to show us the greatest example of being humble, He became obedient unto death, He suffered, endured and sacrificed a lot for us. And as I stated earlier, even though He was made in the likeness of men, He was still God. Because our Savior was both fully divine and completely human during His earthly life, He could have easily said no to death, but He stayed humble not only to death but even unto His dying on the cross. You see Christ could have said yes to death but no to the cross. He could have chosen an alternate death, perhaps one that was not painful...like dying in His sleep. But again He was obedient to the will of the Father by dying on the cross, suffering all the severely painful afflictions that accompanied that way of death.

Humbling one's self in the manner in which Christ did, is also being obedient, submitted and committed unto God totally and completely. Jesus could have decided not to do this assignment from the Father, again because of Him being in the form of God and equal to God, He could have said no, give it to someone else or let's not do it at all. He could have made any decision He wanted too, however He selected to do the will of the Father.

Although we are not equal to God, it would be so easy for us to say these things too when we don't want to do what we are called to do or when we realize it is not what we thought it would be like or when things seem to hard to bare... However we have to make a conscious decision to trust God in His purpose and His will without question, rather than following our own ideas, thoughts and desires and so on, which is also another part of having the mind of Christ.

Results...

Because of our Lord's mindset, it allowed Him to stay the course that God, the Father set for Him while He was on this earth. If we let that same mindset be in us, then we too can have the strength to stay on course, and know that our reward will be great in heaven but also know that we can live the life that God has designed for us full of blessings from above. Let not our reasons for serving be about the blessings or about "what am I going to get out of this" but about the fact that God has awesomely shown that He loves us with His ultimate sacrifice and the most unselfish show of love, our Savior's dying on the cross. Therefore we should do all that is needed to the best of our abilities, to in return show our love to Him!

Because of all that our Lord did and the manner in which He did it, God rewarded Him greatly by highly exalting Him and giving Him a name above all names! There is no name greater and we should recognize, honor and show our appreciation and thanks. That is why it says "that at the name of Jesus every knee should bow" and the part which says "of things in heaven" I believe it is referring to the decisions that were made there which lead to our salvation, as well as heaven itself. "And things in earth" refers to all that was accomplished by this great deed along with all that our Lord has given us in this earth. "And that every tongue should confess that Jesus Christ is Lord" we should be shouting this out in praise, adoration and celebration with thanks giving! "To the glory of God the Father" because of what He's done for us.

Recap...

Having the mindset of Christ is:

➢ A commandment from God for our daily way of living
➢ You electing to make the conscious choice to do the will of the Father
➢ Emptying yourself so that God can fill you up with His purpose
➢ Having the attitude of a true servant without murmuring or complaining
➢ Submitting totally and completely to the WILL of God
➢ Being humble
➢ Being obedient unto God's will
➢ Conditioning our heart to stay the course
➢ Having a willingness to serve God and others
➢ Being 100% committed unto God
➢ Trusting God WITHOUT question
➢ A selfless action done not out of a "what am I going to get out of it" attitude
➢ The ultimate show of true love toward mankind, let it be shown in our actions towards others
➢ Results are God will GREATLY reward you and HIGHLY bless you!

LET'S CELEBRATE AND GIVE GOD THE GLORY!

CHAPTER 19

SPIRITUAL EXERCISE WILL MAKE
YOUR STAYING POWER ATTAINABLE

I Timothy 4:7-9

7 But refuse profane and old wives' fables, and exercise thyself rather unto Godliness.

8 For bodily exercise profiteth little: but Godliness is profitable unto all things, having promise of the life that now is, and of that which is to come.

9 This is a faithful saying and worthy of all acceptation.

Philippians 3:13-15

13 Brethren, I count not myself to have apprehended: but this one thing I do, forgetting those things which are behind, and reaching forth unto those things which are before,

14 I press toward the mark for the prize of the high calling of God in Christ Jesus.

How do we get off of the life rollercoaster? You know the one we all experience, just as I've shared in this book. Why do we have a difficult time keeping our minds and hearts where they need to be spiritually on an even keel or on going basis?

I feel that the opening scriptures address this in a profound way. Picture this; you decide you want to take up an exercise routine so you decide you are going to walk. You start out walking and find you can only make it a few blocks before you have to stop. But you are determined to get better and better at this, because you know in the long run you'll see healthy results. The next week you find you can do half a mile then with more consistency you find yourself up to one mile than five, than ten miles and so on. Along the way you realize that you're walking distances just gets easier and easier. It is almost like second nature to you, you can barely remember the struggles you had in the very beginning. You have developed a regular routine of bodily exercise. And now you see the physical results of that and you're determined to make this a permanent part of your lifestyle. It's healthy and it's good for you...

Well in order to build a healthy spiritual lifestyle, we have to first understand that it may be hard in the beginning just like in the above example, but with determination and Godly instruction we train ourselves to get stronger and stronger. So when we fall short and maybe backslide or get in a mental slump etc. but then get back up and "come back to ourselves" and do the things we are called to do (number one live a lifestyle full of Godliness) we still move forward. And in time as we practice our spiritual exercise, we notice we seem to go longer periods without getting off track. When we do get off track, it's now for shorter periods of time.

We are training ourselves to be in excellent spiritual condition! Just like in a race on your mark, pressing forward to reach the finish line mark, for the prize of the high calling of God. Before we know it, we are no longer on that spiritual rollercoaster of life. Yet just as any person in training will tell you, we also know that we must keep up our spiritual routine to remain in this excellently healthy mindset.

When we can work our way to this state of mind and daily living, we can more effectively be the men and women who God desires for us to be. We can also enjoy the promise of this life and of that which is to come.

Romans 8:6-8

6 For to be carnally (carnal-of the flesh/body or sensual/sexual) minded is death; but to be spiritually minded is life and peace.

7 Because the carnal mind is enmity(a hostility or hate) against God: for it is not subject to the law of God, neither indeed can be.

8 So then they that are in the flesh cannot please God.

I Timothy 4:6-16

6 If thou put the brethren in remembrance of these things, thou shalt be a **good minister** of Jesus Christ, nourished up in the words of faith and of good doctrine, whereunto thou hast attained.

7 But refuse profane and old Wives' fables, and **exercise** thyself rather unto Godliness.

8 For bodily exercise profiteth little: but Godliness is **profitable** unto all things, having **promise** of the life that now is, and of that which is to come.

9 This is a faithful saying and worthy of all acceptation.

10 For therefore we both labour and suffer reproach, because we trust in the living God, who is the Saviour of all men, specially of those that believe.

11 These things command and teach.

12 Let no man despise thy youth; but be thou an example of the believers, in word, in conversation, in charity, in spirit, in faith, in purity.

13 Till I come, give attendance to reading, to exhortation, to doctrine.

14 Neglect not the gift that is in thee, which was given thee by prophecy, with the laying on of the hands of the presbytery.

15 **Meditate upon these things; give thyself wholly to them; that thy profiting may appear to all.**

16 **Take heed unto thyself, and unto the doctrine; continue in them: for in doing this <u>thou shalt both save thyself, and them that hear thee.</u>**

CONCLUSION:

ISAIAH 53:5

But he was wounded for our transgressions, he was bruised for our iniquities: the chastisement of our peace was upon him; and with his stripes we are **HEALED!**

I heard God saying...

Stay focused and cut negativity out of your life. I tell people God is getting ready to do something really big like...if you were looking at the ocean then it would be like the size of a tsunami not a regular wave...

I know I am going to be instrumental in bringing people together but not for the purpose they think, but because God desires to show HIS people that **He LOVES THEM**...

He loves you who read this book!

MY THANK YOU'S...

First and foremost thank you to my Lord and Savior who spared my life. My prayer is that I will do your will continuously, God and that I will fulfill your purpose for me on this earth!

Thank you to all the wonderful people who have shown me so much love in this time and to those of you who wrote letters expressing the impact that my ordeal had upon your life. Words will never be able to express how much I appreciate each and every one of you. I would name each one of you personally right here on this page, however there just isn't enough space! Please know that you hold a very special place in my heart and that I will always remember your kindness.

Thank you to my Pastors, Pastor Lane and Pastor Kelly for all the love, prayer and support you've shown me and for your being there with me at my first court date. And Pastor Kelly for your checking on me (you know your voice & reminders of His word brings me peace). I love you two!

To my Dad-you know that you are my rescuer! You've helped me in so many ways Dad, including paying my car notes during this time. I love you so much and I appreciate the little things and the big things you've done for me. You're an awesome Dad whom I admire and who is blessed with so many gifts and talents from God. Your favorite, Daughter!

My Mom-sorry folks, but I personally have the most awesome, loving, sweetest, beautiful, kindest, inspiration and caring Mom in the whole wide world! She is my baby! Thanks Mom for opening up your home to me and the girls in my time of need and for all the love you've shown me throughout my life and for always believing in me (both you and Dad). Thank you for the impact you have on people that you may not even be aware of, like the impact on the man who attempted to take my life. Which because of you, he did not kill me. Thank you for editing too, love you. Of course, your favorite kid.

To Mignon, Amber, Alicia, Jasmyn and Kayla- My beautiful Daughters! Each one of you has helped me during these days of healing, spiritually, emotionally, physically and mentally. Each one of you has shown me more love than I could ever imagine. The light of God, His love, His wisdom that he's placed in you, not only blesses me, but it will bless the lives of those whom God desires to bring across your paths as you continue to allow Him to use you. I see so many great things in each of you and I am so blessed that God gave all five of you to me. You bring me so much joy. Thank you.

To Raymond-my Son-in-law, whom I call my Son! Thank you for everything and especially for providing my home away from home in the ATL, and a place to stay when we first moved here. Thanks Son, continue to seek God's face in your life and allow him to guide and direct you in all your endeavors.

My Grandsons-Eric, Dionte & Deondre (twins) and Marcel, Granddaughter Kamor and my unborn Granddaughter, the little lights of my life! It's funny how God will even use children. These boys say some of the most inspiring things to me, their wisdom is incredible. The love all of my Grand children shower me with makes my heart smile! They are such a blessing to my life. I love you and thanks to my boys and baby girl and to my unborn grandchild too, you're always in my heart forever and ever!

My Sister's-Karmen who makes me laugh and reminds me of the closeness we shared as children, I've often told her she should be a Writer with her imagination! God started using you from a young age, embrace your gift. LaShawn who is so sweet most of the time (except when she's sleepy, Karmen, Tori, Amber & Alicia too lol). You're like me in ministry, God has given you a gift to impact people, continue to stir up your gift and keep up the good work in your ministry little sis! Thanks to you also for opening up your home for me and the girls and all the other things you've done. Tori, my tallest yet youngest Sister. You and your family are so funny naturally, that if I need a quick fix of "feel better" all I have to do is come over your house! Seriously though you are also a wonderful and sweet Sister too. You have a gift that you have yet to explore, seek God for the answer. I am truly blessed to have each of you and I wouldn't trade you all for a million dollars, a billion well...... maybe (just kidding) and as for my only Brother-Michael, I'm sure if he were here and able to be a support to me in these days, that he would. Love you all.

Thank you to Nathanuel for giving up your room to Auntie!

Thanks to aunt Pam, aunt Cherie, uncle Tony, Anthony, Ebony, Ivory, Sharita, Amir, LaShawn, Nathanuel, Kristopher and D'Metrius for coming to see me in Georgia and for caring about my health. That meant the world to me; I love you all so much!

Thanks to all my other family members for your love, support and prayers!

Thanks to Meding my other Mom, for the times you helped and also gave monetarily. I love you and hope you and my Dad have a blessed, happy and prosperous marriage.

To Rick (My Ex-Husband)-for all the times you've been a listening ear, and the times you've blessed me and helped me. We will forever be life long friends. God bless you and thank you.

To Renee (My Aunt-in-law)-who had been by my side at almost every court date. You've held my hand, wiped away my tears, prayed for me and with me. I will forever be grateful to you. Thank you and know that I love you.

Lonnie Ward-my ATL/FL business associate and caring friend. You were always saving me when I felt I couldn't stay in Michigan for another minute, you were always there rescuing me! Thanks! You know you also inspire me business wise and in life. I see such a wealth of knowledge and wisdom in you. I hope you write your book soon, I know it will bless so many with your wise insight. I'm so blessed that God had us meet and that you saw the gift that God has placed in me. I look forward to our continued success in future business ventures!

John-from New Zealand-another business associate and caring friend! I always say that our God is so amazing in the things he does. John you and I connected from two different parts of this earth, yet God laid it upon your heart to come to Michigan and meet me and my family on September 8th, 2007. This was truly a blessing to me and my family! You are one of the people who inspired me to reach out and tell my story and to develop the website. I thank you so very much for your love, support and encouraging emails! I know we shall be life long friends! God bless you and may He continue to shine His light upon you and your family!

William, Lisa & children-my other family! Thank you for your love, prayers and support. I will forever be grateful to you for so many things, but especially for your sacrifice on Father's day in helping me to move my things from my place of residency and into storage, and also my office furniture as well. And a special thanks to you Will for being that little Brother to me that has encouraged me, listened to me, reminded me of what I already know about our Lord and just plain old been there for me. I also want to thank you for your appreciation and respect for my work as your partner with the play. I love you all so much, thanks.

Thanks to my other Sister, Monica Ann Ross-for being a listening ear, supporter, encourager, laughter buddy, travel buddy and so on and so on! I love how you let the Holy Spirit guide you and that you are obedient to His will. 'cause when I met you, you were "running with skates on" hahaha Thank you as well for the theme song for HUMS. And for lifting my head up when it's down. I know all your dreams and visions will come to past and be successful, because we serve an Awesome God!

Thank you to Paul, my Brother in Christ for your words of wisdom you shared in this book. We will always be friends and we will always have that special connection we've shared in our many years of knowing each other. Keep up the magnificent work you do for God in your ministry, writing, acting and film work. Love you.

Thank you for the monetary blessing when I first left to go to Atlanta- Will & Lisa, Rick and Carlos.

Thank you to the cast of "Tricks of The Enemy" for your prayers.

Thanks to those from Dunamis Outreach Ministries (my church home)- Lynelle, Elder Linda Harper, Kathy T., Cheryl, Donna, Crystal, Pastor Anderson and others.

Thanks for lending your hands and muscles in my move-Donna, Camaryn, James, Curtis, Heather, Jamilah, Anthony, my kids, My Dunamis family-Deacon Gerald, Tony, Kirk, Crystal's Son Terrell, Will, Lisa & kids, Dave Ivey and the young man on the Praise & Worship team.

Thanks to Chris, My Counselor/Therapist, you have helped me tremendously! I thank God for you, your compassion, your insight, your guidance and your sensitivity to each persons' needs.

Thanks to my Daughter Mignon who briefly was the Public Relations Coordinator for my speaking engagements and interviews. She was also responsible for me having that very first interview with Russ Parr, thanks baby.

My loving Cousins, Chantel, Tina, Devon & Mike! Thank you all for opening up your home to us and for every thing you did, big or small, I appreciate it. I love you all more than mere words can say. When is your next fabulous party darlings, lol!

Thank you Mr. Geary for watching Snow when we had our first annual cruise and to Robert Geary for your help with everything and your donation that made it possible for me to attend. Thanks for the caverns in Tennessee too, Robert.

Thanks to Eric "Big Russ" Russell for your financial and physical labor support and for caring about my Daughters and I.

Thank you Claude "CJ" Johnson Thank God for obedience to the Holy Spirit at the Family Christian Bible store, lol. You have been one of my main supporters here in Georgia in so many ways. I love you and appreciate you so much and I will always remember your kindness.

Thanks to Pastors and Doctors, Mark and Tamara Goodridge for the inspiration and love you showed me and my family while we were in attendance at D.O.M.'s Atlanta church. I will forever be grateful for your kindness.

Thank you Mr. & Mrs. Gary Carter for being the world's greatest Landlords! You two have shown me and my family so much love. May our God continue to bless and prosper your family.

Thank you Ed "Thamelodious" just for being my long distance friend and listening buddy, oh and pokerstars partner, hehehe. Love you.

Thank you to Minister Larry Jones for your Godly insight and for your gracious foreword! May our God continue to use you and shine His heavenly light upon your soul. I'm blessed to have met you.

Thanks to each and every one of the H.U.M.S. volunteers! I love you and thank God for your unselfish help and support because without you, I would not be able to accomplish the things God has purposed for me to do with HUMS.

Thank you to Mikal Crawford for your Pro Bono work with HUMS!

Thanks to those God will send...You will be a key element in the success of HUMS Your work and efforts will result in us getting the word out to our nation and assures the mission of HUMS coming to pass.

Thanks to those who supported HUMS' annual cruise. I appreciate you! Thank you as well who took the time to read this book!

BLESSED
SURVIVOR

ISAIAH 40:31

MY JOURNEY OF SURVIVING ATTEMPTED MURDER + RAPE ON A PURPLE DRIVE

ABOUT THE AUTHOR

BIOGRAPHY

Rhonda Knight is the Founder of Uplifting Hearts, Minds & Souls (H.U.M.S.). As you've read, Ms. Knight is a survivor of attempted murder and rape and is on a mission to make a change in our Nation. She is very dedicated in the fight to help stop violence towards women and very dedicated in all her ministries. She feels that this is a part of her calling and purpose on this earth.

Ms. Knight is a Motivational Speaker/Minister who tells her story of surviving a horrendous attack on her life. She also inspires, educates, encourages and challenges her listeners. Her speaking is from the heart and very touching. She's been heard on several radio shows, one of which was the Russ Parr morning show (nationally syndicated) and several TV shows. She's also spoken on many platforms to a variety of audiences; Schools, Churches, Organizations, Universities, Special Events, For Police Departments, General audiences, Women's groups and an all Men's group!

In addition to the above, she does a series called **"New Beginnings"** which consists of workshops and seminars to help others to improve their quality of life.

New Beginnings list:

A change of heart- The series, presented as a seminar. Spiritually inspirational and motivational!

How to heal and overcome your past/present unhealthy relationships-presented as a workshop.

Moving into a purpose filled life-presented as a workshop.

Empowerment from fear-interactive 2 hr. workshop.

Rhonda says she's a very proud Mother of five beautiful Daughters and four handsome Grandsons, one lovely Granddaughter and a new baby Granddaughter's arrival coming soon!

Ms. Knight is also an Evangelist and says this gift is one that she cherishes in her heart. Not the title but the gift that God has given her. "I hope to live my life as an example I'd rather walk the walk than talk the talk".

Among other things, Ms. Knight has piloted a program called "**Uplifting Neighborhoods**". This project is in two parts, one is a program called "**H.U.M.S. Heroes**" designed to help under privileged children cope with the issues in their neighborhoods. It trains them in Drama which leads into Drama Therapy for healing. The second half of their program emphasizes safety training, mannerisms and helping to beautify the community.

The other, "**H.U.M.S. Hopegivers**" is geared towards women in those communities with programs to help with issues such as domestic violence, dating violence, rape etc. It is a project that trains and empowers these women to eventually run the program themselves. Thus encouraging a cycle of neighbors uplifting each other and building up their communities!

Rhonda had also been a regular and frequent speaker as well as mentor at Vista Maria, a fairly large girl's juvenile facility located in Michigan. "Sadly the majority of these girls have been victims themselves which more than likely attributes to their acting out" she exclaims.

She plans to produce the television show "**Uplifting**" which she will host. The show gives a voice to survivors and is comprised of expert panelists. Its unique design is formatted to inform and educate this nation's viewing audience and to encourage community involvement. it is also structured to deal with cultural and/or religious challenges victims may face.

She is the sole Author of this novel "BLESSED SURVIVOR –My journey from survival of attempted murder and rape to a purpose filled life" Ms. Knight is excited to embark upon a **2011 6 months NATIONAL speaking and book signing tour** to promote this book. The national tour includes a week of engagements in 23 states and then ends in New Zealand and Australia!

She is presently penning a sequel to "**BLESSED SURVIVOR**" entitled:

"LOOK HOW FAR GOD'S BROUGHT ME FROM-Walking in the blessings of God"

Previously to her speaking professionally, Ms. Knight enjoyed an extensive career as an Actor, Writer, Director, Producer, Professional Theatrical Makeup Artist and Instructor of Drama. She has experience in the technical aspect of theatre too as a Technical Director and Lighting Technician and doing basic sound as well. Because of owning her own production company, it equipped her to be successful in producing, marketing, advertising and promoting. With a chuckle she exclaims she's even done clowning and professional face painting! She states she still performs and is available for any of these noted positions as well.

To book **Ms. Knight visit:** **www.bookrhondaknight.com**

Part of the proceeds from book sells goes to H.U.M.S. To further support the cause, Uplifting Hearts, Minds & Souls please visit our website:

www.h-u-m-s.org

E-Store: www.rhondaknight.com

Email: Rhonda_Knight@h-u-m-s.org

Lady Knight Enterprises Publishing 678 667-2311

www.ladyknightenterprisespublishing.com